TWAYNE'S WORLD LEADERS SERIES

EDITORS OF THIS VOLUME

Arthur W. Brown
*Baruch College, The City University
of New York*
and
Thomas S. Knight
Adelphi University

Ananda K. Coomaraswamy

TWLS 75

Ananda K. Coomaraswamy

ANANDA K. COOMARASWAMY

By VISHWANATH S. NARAVANE

TWAYNE PUBLISHERS
A DIVISION OF G. K. HALL & CO., BOSTON

Library of Congress Cataloging in Publication Data

Naravane, Vishwanath S
Ananda K. Coomaraswamy.

(Twayne's world leaders series ; TWLS 75)
Bibliography: p. 169–181
Includes index.
1.   Coomaraswamy, Ananda Kentish, 1877-1947—
Addresses, essays, lectures.
DS435.7.c66N37   700'.92'4   78–5580
ISBN 0–8057–7722–9

To the Memory of My Sister

Malati

Contents

About the Author

Vishwanath S. Naravane was born at Allahabad, India, in 1922. He obtained his Ph.D. in 1946 from the University of Allahabad, where he joined the faculty as Assistant Professor of Philosophy — a position which he held for eighteen years. From 1965 to 1968 he was Professor and Chairman of the Department of Philosophy at the University of Poona. In recent years Professor Naravane has lectured in various parts of the world, and has given courses in Philosophy, Religion, Art and Literature at several well-known American colleges and Universities. His publications include *Modern Indian Thought: A Philosophical Survey, The Elephant and the Lotus: Essays in Philosophy and Culture,* and *An Introduction to Rabindranath Tagore.*

Preface

The writings of Ananda K. Coomaraswamy have had a powerful impact on two generations of orientalists. In recent years his influence has extended far beyond academic circles. And yet there is hardly any book giving a systematic assessment of Coomaraswamy as a man, a scholar, and a thinker. The present volume is a humble attempt to fill, at least partially, this surprising lacuna in modern scholarship. The attempt seems particularly appropriate in 1977, the year which marks the centenary of his birth.

I would like to emphasize, however, that this work is not intended to be of merely topical interest, even though it is being published on the occasion of the Coomaraswamy Centennial. It is being offered as a serious — though brief — study of an important figure in such diverse fields as philosophy, religion, art, literature, and cultural history.

During the period when this book was being written, many American scholars helped me in different ways. I am grateful to all of them. In particular, I wish to express my thankfulness to the following friends: Professor Robert McDermott of Baruch College, New York; Professor Thomas Hopkins of Franklin and Marshall College, Lancaster, Pennsylvania; Professor John Hutchison of the Claremont Graduate School, California; Dean E.C. Reckard and Dr. Gordon C. Winsor of Centre College, Kentucky; Professor Austin B. Creel of the University of Florida, Gainesville; Professor Jack D. Van Horn of the College of William and Mary, Williamsburg, Virginia; Professor William David and Dr. Ira Zepp of the Western Maryland College, Westminster, Maryland; and Professor George Parker of Berea College, Kentucky.

I am grateful to Dr. Rama P. Coomaraswamy who kindly gave me permission to use a photograph of his illustrious father.

Like many other researchers I have profited immensely from the advice and assistance of Shri Durai Raja Singam of Malaysia. My debt to him can hardly be expressed through formal acknowledgment. Totally indifferent to publicity or financial gain, this noble

ANANDA K. COOMARASWAMY

and humble scholar has dedicated half a century to the study of Coomaraswamy's life and work. Many years ago, when I visited Shri Singam's house at Petaling Jaya, a suburb of Kuala Lumpur, he generously placed at my disposal his enormous knowledge and experience. Since then he has constantly encouraged me in various ways, and I have turned to him for help in tracking down many an obscure reference. The bibliography at the end of this book is the result of Shri Durai Raja Singam's patient labor, though I have abridged it slightly and made a few minor changes in the arrangement of the material.

VISHWANATH S. NARAVANE

'Shanti Nivas'
Allahabad, U.P., India.

Chronology

1834 Muthu Coomaraswamy, the father of Ananda Coomaraswamy, born in Shri Lankā.

1875 Muthu Coomaraswamy marries Elizabeth Clay Beeby.

1877 Ananda Coomaraswamy born on August 22.

1879 Death of Muthu Coomaraswamy. Ananda and his mother go to England.

1886 Ananda admitted to Wycliffe School.

1897 Ananda returns to Shri Lankā for a brief visit.

1900 Coomaraswamy secures B.Sc. from University College, London, with Honours in Geology and Botany.

1902– Director of the Geological Survey of Ceylon. Studies effects
1906 of technology on traditional crafts.

1906 First journey to India.

1907 Association with C. R. Ashbee and Eric Gill in the movement for the preservation of indigenous handicrafts in Gloucestershire.

1910- Travels in India.
1911

1911 In charge of the Art Section at the United Provinces Exhibition at Allahabad in India.

1914 Coomaraswamy meets Mahatma Gandhi in London.

1917 Appointed Keeper of the Indian Section at the Museum of Fine Arts, Boston.

1920 Journey to Java and Cambodia.

1922 Islamic Art added to the section of the Museum of Fine Arts placed in charge of Coomaraswamy.

1924 Founder-President of India Culture Center at New York.

1938 President of the National Committee for India's Freedom.

1941 Foundation of the East-West Association at New York.

1947 India and Pakistan become independent nations (August 15). Coomaraswamy delivers an address at Harvard to mark the event.

1947 August 22. Farewell address at the Harvard Club.

1947 September 8. Death of Ananda Coomaraswamy.

CHAPTER 1

Introduction

I would like to begin this essay by recalling a conversation with an American scholar who was my guest in India several years ago. We had just returned home after a visit to the local museum. As we settled down for leisurely conversation over a pot of tea, my friend fell into a reminiscent mood. He told me of the phases of discouragement through which he had passed in his earliest attempts to come to grips with the Indian cultural tradition. The vastness of the material had overwhelmed him. He had often lost his way in the forest of ideas that had grown in the course of forty centuries. When I asked how he had managed to overcome his discouragement he said, "I was saved by the golden rule: 'when in difficulty, go to Coomaraswamy.' Now whenever I feel that something is beyond my reach I just climb on Coomaraswamy's shoulders and get there."

The reply struck me as an apt description of what I had myself experienced on innumerable occasions. Indeed, it would be difficult to find, in the field of contemporary oriental scholarship, any serious researcher who has not, at one point or another, gone to Ananda Coomaraswamy's writings for guidance. I would, however, like to vary my friend's metaphor. The image of mounting Coomaraswamy's shoulders, expressive though it is, does not reveal the full extent of our debt to him. His work does much more than give us a higher vantage point or enable us to extend our reach. It is like a magic ladder which not only lengthens itself but also carries us from shelf to shelf pointing to hidden places we had forgotten to explore. Sometimes this miraculous ladder even deliberately pulls us down when we climb too high and shows us that the most precious objects of our search may well be in the bottom drawer. Whatever our starting-point — philosophy or religion,

13

mythology or poetry, art or archaeology — Coomaraswamy leads us from one sphere to another with perfect naturalness until our insight becomes not only clearer but also more unified.

This is precisely where Coomaraswamy's achievement is unique. It is possible to think of other scholars whose knowledge was equally encyclopedic; but it is difficult to name another who has clarified the relationships between the major disciplines of human civilization as consistently and vividly as Coomaraswamy has done. He does this without resorting to catchphrases or high-sounding rhetoric, unraveling the strands of thought, calmly, patiently. He deals with specific issues with all the zeal, expertise and single-minded attention of a trained specialist. But he never forgets that every important question, statement, attitude, or concept is embedded in a larger pattern which gives it meaning. In Coomaraswamy's writings we feel, in every paragraph, the author's insatiable thirst for meaning, for the inner significance which lies behind the data which he collects from a variety of sources with almost incredible toil. That is why, when we read his comments on a work of art, or a philosophical system, or an ancient legend, we experience not only a widening but also a deepening and a heightening of our consciousness. As an example of the effect which his exposition of any theme produces upon the reader's mind, the following comment made by an outstanding orientalist is worthy of note. Referring to Coomaraswamy's *Buddhist Iconography* this scholar says, "His explanation of motifs transfers them from the category of the ornamental to the category of the significant."[1]

Some one has described Ananda Coomaraswamy as the perfect prototype of the pure scholar. But what do we mean by the phrase "pure scholarship"? If it implies the pursuit of knowlege in a spirit of selfless dedication, the description is accurate. He was wholly free from prejudice, arrogance, envy and other "impurities" — to use a traditional religious expression — which have stained the work of many a pundit. But if we regard a pure scholar as one for whom knowledge is an end in itself, the ultimate goal of all endeavor, Coomaraswamy cannot be placed in such a category. For him, as for all the great exponents of the traditional view which he accepted wholeheartedly, knowledge was *not* its own reward but merely a preparation for that state of harmony in which both knowing and doing (or "making") are inseparable from being.[2] As we shall see in detail in subsequent chapters of this book, all his writings are marked by the conviction that this view of knowledge was once universally accepted by men of all vocations; and that the repudiation of this view in the West was the starting point of the conflicts between nations, creeds, ideologies, and cultures which have darkened the history of mankind during the last five centuries. From this point of view it would perhaps be better to characterize Ananda Coomaraswamy as a creative scholar rather than a pure scholar. This distinction needs to be stressed, because all too often he is praised almost exclusively for his erudition, his mastery of languages, the stupendous range of his equipment. Ironically enough, such praise sometimes comes from those who have altogether missed the main point of Coomaraswamy's work and have failed to grasp the deeper significance of his researches. His energy and skill were not expended merely in bringing to light bits and pieces and putting them together. The pieces were not just assembled; they were fused into an integral whole. The explorer was also the interpreter. Analysis was invariably a stepping-stone to synthesis. One of his disciples has put the matter admirably in these words: "His brilliant observations . . . were a *making,* not a recording. He heard and saw in a processs of creation, not re-creation, just as Kashyapa saw the true meaning of the lotus in the hand of the Buddha."[3]

It is thus that he should be remembered in the year of his birth centenary: as one who *saw,* in the deepest sense of the word *seeing.* On the twenty-second of August, 1977, tributes will be paid to Coomaraswamy all over the world, particularly in India, Shri Lankā,[4] and the United States — the three countries which meant so much to him and his work. But if these tributes are not to remain a mere formality, an earnest attempt must be made to follow his gaze in the realm of meaning. Coomaraswamy's search for meaning was not just a logical or semantic endeavor. It was that, but it was also much more. As we read his essays we find ourselves in the presence of a man who peels the world of fact and events, layer by layer, until he can lay his hand upon that which illumines, beautifies, and ennobles the sum total of experience. A true disciple of Plato, he tried to comprehend things in the light of eternity. The goal which he had set for himself must be kept in view if we are to get from Coomaraswamy's writings that which is most valuable. We may occasionally disagree with his interpretations. But unless we understand his perspective we will reap a very poor harvest from the prodigious labor which he expended on our behalf. A casual or complacent reader cannot do justice to his genius.[5] Let us, at least on this point, accept the ancient Indian tradition which was so dear to him; let us acknowledge that to approach a qualified teacher the pupil must first qualify himself.

In the present work I will try to present the main ideas of Ananda Coomaraswamy as reflecting a unified world view. A study of his ideas, however, involves a familiarity with his scholarly equipment and stylistic habits; and these, in turn, can hardly be appreciated without looking at the human side of his personality: his nurture and education, tastes and interests, travels and friendships, and influences which molded his mind and character. The next two chapters will be devoted to a study of Ananda Coomaraswamy as a *person* and as a *scholar* respectively. These will be followed by an account of his philosophical, religious, aesthetic, social and educational views. Comment and criticism will be deferred until the concluding chapter. But before I proceed to follow this plan it seems appropriate to state briefly the chief attainments which have earned him such a unique place in the world of modern scholarship. Some of the issues raised in the remainder of this introductory chapter will be taken up in greater detail in subsequent portions of the book. My intention at this point is merely to summarize his distinctive contributions so as to place my study in an intelligible focus.

I   *Interpretation of India for the West*

In the first place, we have to consider Coomaraswamy's success in interpreting the East, and especially India, to the West. He was not the first to make such an attempt. At the beginning of the nineteenth century Ram Mohan Roy tried to present India's religious heritage in such a way that British scholars, educationists and reformers might be able to appreciate and understand it.[6] But Ram Mohan, like all pioneers, had to work under serious limitations. Moreover, much of his time and energy were spent in countering the attacks of Christian missionaries on the one hand and Indian orthodoxy on the other. Towards the end of the nineteenth century Swami Vivekananda, through his dynamic activities and his eloquent exposition of Hinduism, carried on the process of projecting Indian culture in a favorable light.[7] Among Coomaraswamy's contemporaries, Sarvepalli Radhakrishnan continued the dialogue.[8] But all these spokesmen confined their attention only to the religious and philosophical side of India's cultural history. Rabindranath Tagore and Ananda Coomaraswamy went much further. They looked at the Indian tradition in its entirety, and the image of India which they presented to the West was therefore much more vivid. Both Tagore and Coomaraswamy were cultural ambassadors in the finest sense of the term. The former through his lectures[9] and his creative work, and the latter through his profound elucidations, focused attention on the strongest and the most enduring aspects of the tradition. And they did so without mawkish sentimentality. In evaluating Ananda Coomaraswamy's work in this field we are struck by the fact that, unlike many others who have written in praise of India, he is neither dogmatic nor apologetic.[10] He does not attempt to prove India's inherent superiority, nor does he resort to sophistry in order to whitewash the darker side of Indian life. He does not write as a sectarian and shows no partiality towards any particular religious or regional expression of Indian culture.[11] Hinduism, Buddhism, Jainism, Islam, Sikhism, Christianity, and the local and tribal cults that have arisen from time to time: all these are taken into account. Like Tagore, Coomaraswamy looks upon the culture of the Indian subcontinent as a river which becomes broader as it flows towards the sea, gathering up and absorbing within its current the waters of all its tributaries.[12] He does not limit his gaze to ancient India. Illustrations in support of his formulations are derived from medieval as well as modern developments in all the fields of culture.[13]

II *Interpretation of India for Indians*

Coomaraswamy not only interprets India to the West but also to Indians themselves. His criticism is leveled not only against the Westerners who misunderstand or distort what India has stood for but also against Indians who are ignorant of their heritage or glorify it for the wrong reasons. Indeed, the latter are taken to task more severely than the former. He presents to his readers and hearers in India — and in Shri Lankā, which he considers an intrinsic part of India spiritually and culturally[14] — a picture which is not only attractive but also lucid and intelligible. He exhorts his countrymen to understand the deeper meaning of the beliefs and institutions, rituals and ceremonies, preferences or inhibitions, which they often accept without comprehension or reject in an equally superficial manner. He asks them never to reject anything simply because it is alien or to accept anything simply because it has the sanction of usage; to discriminate between essentials and inessentials, between the inner spirit and the outward injunctions, between the traditional and the merely customary. Coomaraswamy's attempt to interpret the East for the orientals, India for the Indians, began with his very first lectures in Shri Lankā as early as 1905. It continued throughout his life. Only three weeks before his death, on the occasion of India's attainment of national freedom, he made some extremely significant observations regarding the possibilities that had opened up for India.[15] He warned against the tendency of viewing national freedom only in terms of political or economic issues. The future reconstruction of the country, he pointed out, could only be undertaken on the basis of a thorough grasp of the fundamental basis of Indian life and culture.

III   *Interpretation of the Western Tradition*

Coomaraswamy also strove for a correct and balanced estimate of the Western tradition. He was as much an interpreter of the West for the West as he was of the East for the East, and of each for the other. While he criticized *modern* Western civilization, he repeatedly pointed out that in ancient and medieval times the West had achieved all those insights which are enshrined in the oriental religions and philosophies. Even with regard to the modern age, he gave credit where credit was due and pointed to the work of many outstanding Western scholars and thinkers.[16] Coomaraswamy did not ask the West to orientalize itself but merely to return to the nobler part of its own heritage. There are two Wests: the metaphysical, which is heir to universal and imperishable truths and which employs science in the service of those truths; and the industrial, which is aggressive, intolerant, and arrogant and which has deviated from the main stream which once animated and sustained all that was good and elevating in it. It is only the latter which he condemned. For the former — the West of Plato and Augustine, of Philo and Marcus Aurelius, of Meister Eckhart and Ambrose, of Blake and Nietzsche, of Eric Gill and Rene Guenon — he had nothing but reverence. In his interpretation of the West, Coomaraswamy questioned some of the basic assumptions from which modern technological society derives its ethical and aesthetic assessments and organizes its educational system. These assumptions are: that complexity is the mark of progress; that spiritual criteria cannot and should not be applied to social, political and economic questions; that the intellect is the highest source of knowledge; that there is no connection between what is useful and what is beautiful;

that freedom consists in self-expression or in the ability to "do what one pleases." A further assumption — the most dangerous of all — is that all these assumptions should be foisted upon those communities which have thus far remained unaffected by them, because that is the only way in which the blessings of civilization can be bestowed upon them.[17] Coomaraswamy calls upon the West to reexamine these assumptions and join hands in the task of restoring to human life that harmony which its aggressive attitudes have interrupted.

IV *Internationalism*

Coomaraswamy emerges from his writings as one of the great internationalists of our age. This side of his work is obscured by the fact that he is often described primarily as an ardent admirer of everything Indian. Actually, he was completely free from national partisanship. There is not a trace of chauvinism in his evaluation of other cultures. Born in Ceylon, educated in England, settled in the United States, he regarded India as his spiritual home. But one of the strongest features of the ancient Indian ideal, in his judgment, was its cosmopolitanism. The religion of the Upanishads was not for any chosen people. Long before any other people had even vaguely conceived of international brotherhood, the sages of ancient India spoke of the "world as one family" (*vasudhaiva kutumbakam*) and dreamed of a condition in which "the entire universe becomes a single nest" (*yatra vishvam bhavati ekanidam*). Criticizing the narrow nationalism of some of his Indian contemporaries, Coomaraswamy drew attention to this broad-minded and assimilative approach of their ancestors.[18]

Coomaraswamy's search was for the common denominators between the cultures of all lands. While pointing out the differences, he viewed them as necessary variants of human expression which have helped to save unity from uniformity. His vast erudition, his knowledge of many Eastern and Western languages, the experience gained through extensive travel throughout the world, and his personal contacts with scholars, artists and thinkers of many countries: all these assets were employed in demonstrating the fundamental unity of the major faiths that have inspired mankind. But his search for a meeting ground between diverse peoples was not confined to the study of religion alone. It was also based on a study of literatures, art styles, myths, customs and beliefs, even handi-

crafts. His exposition of the "Perennial Philosophy," grounded
upon a tradition that was once universal, is his most enduring contribution to the cause of human unity.

V   *Appreciation of Folk Culture*

Coomaraswamy's work shows his remarkable ability to identify
with the common man's point of view. Although he spent much of
his time in the seclusion of his office, engaged in highly specialized
researches, he did not develop an ivory tower mentality. In all his
writings he insists upon the close and continuous connection
between the folk and classical forms of culture. No other scholar of
our times has devoted so much attention to popular music, painting, and poetry, or studied with such insight the beliefs, customs,
and modes of worship of ordinary men and women. In these he
found the reflection — sometimes hazy or distorted, but always
interesting — of ideas deeply rooted in a tradition which was once
universally accepted. His observations on primitive cultures opened
many new lineš of research and corrected the glaring flaws in some
anthropological theories.[19] Instead of looking upon primitive communities as uncivilized or stagnant, he regards them as preservers
of many valuable elements in art, religion, and social organization.
Coomaraswamy's approach to popular culture is free from condescension and from the tendency to evaluate everything in terms of
the assumptions of modern technological society, which mars the
work of many of his contemporaries. He does not glorify the noble
savage, because to him the primitive communities that have sur-
vived are not savage societies but simply groups of men who are in
the declining phase of a once sophisticated civilization. As for
stagnation, he points out that modern man, with his obsession with
change and movement and his confusion between progress and
complexity, is apt to condemn a life-style as stagnant because he
has made himself incapable of understanding the value of harmony
or contentment. Coomaraswamy also draws attention to some of
the positive features of folk culture — keenness of observation,
uncanny sense of rhythm, a sensitiveness to color and sound which
does not depend on theoretical training, an instinctive skill in
combining utility with beauty, and a perfect attunement to the.phe-
nomena of nature.

VI   *Modernity and Scientific Outlook*
I now turn to an aspect of Coomaraswamy's work which needs

particularly to be emphasized because it has been neglected: his fundamentally modern and scientific outlook. His advocacy of the *Philosophia Perennis* and his condemnation of certain features of contemporary industrial societies led some of his critics to dub him as unscientific. Others even labelled him as a medievalist. But a close look at his writings will convince any objective reader that his approach is logical and rational throughout his exposition of the theme he handles, *up to the point where logic and reason can go*. To say that there is a transcendental mode of being which can only be experienced but not analyzed through the categories of the intellect is not unscientific. Coomaraswamy used all the resources of modern science in his research. He was thoroughly familiar with the latest developments in archaeology, linguistics, and anthropology. If we compare his writings with the utterances of some of the gurus and swamis of the present generation[20] we can easily see the real difference between mystification, which is anti-scientific, and mysticism, which is simply the recognition of the limits of scientific enquiry.[21] There is nothing vague, ambiguous, or effusive about Coomaraswamy's exposition. To trace every concept to its sources, to elucidate the meaning of every term in strict accordance with etymology, to cite chapter and verse in support of every assertion, to assess every art work only after a thorough study of photographic, palaeographic, or geological evidence — surely all these point to a scientific attitude, even if the conclusion reached is in support of a metaphysic of Absolute Idealism. Coomaraswamy does not reject science in favor of metaphysics. He recognizes the validity of science at the empirical, phenomenal level. He only rejects the claim that the methods of natural science are the only sources of knowledge, and he condemns the use of scientific techniques in a manner which destroys man's harmony with the universe in which he dwells.

Just as there is no necessary conflict between science on the one hand and metaphysics or religion on the other, so also "modernity" in the true sense of the term does not consist in belittling the attainments of bygone ages or glorifying the new simply because it is new. A writer or critic who looks upon the Middle Ages as one long stretch of darkness and superstition is not really being modern. On the contrary he is showing himself to be out of date.[22] Even the philosopher who thinks that metaphysics has outlived its worthwhileness and that philosophical enquiry consists only in the analysis of meanings is already becoming obsolete even though he may

have appeared modern a decade ago. Ananda Coomaraswamy
interprets modernity as an attitude of tolerance and understanding
born out of increased knowledge, an attitude of sympathy resulting
from the improvements in the means of communication and travel
that have brought different peoples and cultures closer to each
other. He repeatedly asserts that his acceptance of the traditional
philosophy does not imply revivalism. The value of an idea, a work
of art or an institution is to be judged not in the light of whether it
was produced in antiquity, or in the twelfth century, or in the
nineteen-fifties. The real criterion is whether it promoted human
happiness in its own times, and whether it contains something
which is true for all time.

In brief, one of Coomaraswamy's significant contributions is to
show that one can accept a traditional philosophy and speak from
an orthodox point of view, while at the same time reflecting the
rationalism of science and the universalism of the modern age.

VII   *Some Anticipations*

Another important feature of Coomaraswamy's work is that in
almost every field of scholarship he put forward hypotheses which
were subsequently verified, made discoveries whose significance
was realized a few decades later, and anticipated criticism of
theories which appeared well established but were later found to be
erroneous or inaccurate. This will become clear when we discuss his
views on philosophy, religion, art, and education in appropriate
chapters of this book. But a few examples may be mentioned here.
In his essays on the cultural history of India, Coomaraswamy
pointed out the pre-Aryan origin of many ideas, attitudes, rituals,
even myths and symbols, which had been traditionally assigned to
the Vedic Age. In most cases his views proved correct in the light of
evidence which became available later. His assessment of the Indus
Valley Civilization also shows sound judgment. The artifacts
yielded by the Harappa excavations had not yet been finally dated,
and there were many unanswered questions about the origin of the
Indus Valley culture, the causes of its decline, and the religious
beliefs of the people who evolved it. But Coomaraswamy came to
correct conclusions on three important points: that the Harappan
culture was indigenous to the Indian subcontinent and was not a
mere offshoot of the Sumerian, that its influence extended far
beyond the Indus valley, and that the people of the Indus Valley

had close links with the Dravidian races of southern India.

Coomaraswamy was among the first to grasp the significance of Hindu mythology as a vital link between the metaphysical concepts of the philosophers and the ethical-religious ideals of the common people. He stressed the continuity between the Hindu and the Buddhist traditions at a time when it was fashionable among Indologists to consider Buddhism as a revolt against Brahmanical orthodoxy. He showed that the Buddha, contrary to popular belief, did *not* reject the Self (Atman) of the Upanishads; that Nirvana does *not* mean "extinction" in the ultimate sense;[23] that the Buddha image was created by the Mathura and *not* the Gandhara school; that the Shūnyavā[24] school of Mahāyāna does *not* imply nihilism; that transmigration in the orthoodx sense does *not* mean the return of individual personalities to corporeal life on earth; that the so-called Bhakti Movement[25] did *not* emerge as a sectarian trend in the Middle Ages but was implicit in elements of religious thought which go back to the second century before Christ; that the Rajput School of miniature painting is *not* just a branch or a style of the Mughal School but an independent expression of ancient Indian norms.[26]

I am not suggesting that Coomaraswamy was the first to put forward these views in *every* case, or that he has been proved correct on *all* these issues. But he was undeniably a pioneer in many fields and the first to discover the value of some hitherto obscure works of art (Pahari miniatures, for instance).[27] On all the points mentioned above he adhered to views which were at first acceptable only to a few, and it was largely through his influence that the minority was later converted into the majority.

VIII   *Aesthetic Orientation*

Finally, and in some ways most important of all, it is Coomaraswamy's special contribution to have given an aesthetic direction to every field of study that he touched. The similarity between Coomaraswamy and Tagore is again apparent. And once again it should be pointed out that while Tagore' aesthetic emphasis came largely through his own creative work in literature and music, Coomaraswamy gave an aesthetic orientation to oriental and medieval European studies through his sensitive exposition of the creative work of all ages and countries and his elucidation of the profound thoughts which inspired it. Apart from his special contribution to the study of art and aesthetics, his approach to metaphysics, ethics, social thought and education reflects his aesthetic predilection quite clearly. He regarded the *Philosophia Perennis* not only as universally true but also as abidingly beautiful. His grievance against contemporary technological society was not only that it was superficial and lacked a sound philosophical basis and that it led to cynicism towards ethical principles, but also that it separated utility from beauty and deprived human life of its harmony, grace and loveliness. Even as a nationalist he was less concerned with political dominance and economic exploitation than with the harm that foreign rule had done to Eastern nations by corrupting the taste of their people and destroying the feeling for perfection and beauty which their artists and craftsmen once possessed. In his interpretation of the major religious traditions — especially Buddhism, Hinduism, and medieval Christianity — he gave as much attention to their aesthetic expressions as to their ethical principles or practical injunctions. And in his educational views the aesthetic motif is apparent in almost all his writings.

In an age when philosophy was turning its back upon the richness of human experience and concerning itself increasingly with the analysis of logical propositions, when politics was becoming cynical and sociologists were bypassing the spiritual element in life in favor of purely materialistic criteria, when art was becoming formal, impersonal and abstract, Ananda Coomaraswamy brought to modern throught a grace, a sophistication, and a feeling for harmony and beauty which were sorely needed.

CHAPTER 2

The Man and His Background

L IKE a devotee's hands folded in prayer, the two coastlines of
India meet at the southern extremity of the subcontinent and
offer their homage to the Indian Ocean. And not too far away,
separated from the mainland only by a few miles, the island of Shri
Lankā glistens like a precious emerald set in the silver sea. This
delightful island, known in the Western world by its popular name,
Ceylon, has been linked with India by historical and cultural ties
which go back to the fifth century before Christ. The climactic
scene of the *Ramayana* was enacted here. And it was to this legendary region, which the ancients called Simhala or Tambapanni, that
the great Emperor Ashoka, Beloved of the Gods, sent his son
Mahendra to spread the Buddha's message. Shri Lankā thus
became the first country outside India where the Wheel of the Law
was set in motion two centuries after the Tathagata attained
parinirvāna.

Shri Lankā did not, however, remain a mere adjunct of India. It
evolved its own language and life-style. Its talented and industrious
inhabitants created a national tradition in the arts and crafts. Nor
was Shri Lankā always India's debtor. Many texts of the Theravāda
school of Buddhism would have perished if they had not been preserved in Sinhalese — the language of Shri Lankā — and later
retranslated into Pali. And the Bodhi Tree at Gayā, under which
Prince Siddhārta sought and won Enlightenment, would have left
no descendants had not a sapling been taken to Shri Lankā. Sinhalese Buddhists reared the sapling with devotion; and the lineage of
the Tree of Wisdom was preserved from generation to generation
until, a few centuries later, a sapling was taken from Shri Lankā to
Gayā and planted at the exact spot where the Budda had meditated.

In the family of Ananda Coomaraswamy both these features of

the Sinhalese tradition found expression: its distinctiveness as well as its affinity with India. The name Coomaraswamy refers to Kumāra,[1] one of the important figures in the Hindu pantheon. Kumāra, also known as Skanda or Kārtikeya, was a son of Shiva. It was expressly for the purpose of begetting Kumāra, who was destined to rid the world of a wicked demon, that Shiva, the Great Ascetic, was persuaded to marry Pārvati. Kālidāsa's *Kumārasambhavam* ("Birth of Kumara"), the greatest poem in classical Sanskrit literature, is based on this theme.[2] The origin of the family name, Coomaraswamy, is sometimes traced to a goddess called Kumāri, whose sanctuary was located near Kanyākumāri (Cape Camorin). Be that as it may, the Coomaraswamys were Hindus. But we must hasten to add that Ananda and his father always expressed deep reverence for the Buddha and firmly believed that there was no divergence beteen Hinduism and Buddhism on fundamentals. They were equally conversant with Sanskrit and Pali; and both Tamil and Sinhalese were used in their home. The Coomaraswamys regarded Shri Lankā as their motherland and identified themselves with the national aspirations of that country, but they never ceased to emphasize that India and Shri Lankā shared a common spiritual and aesthetic idiom.

I   *Parents*

Ananda's grandfather, Mudaliyar Coomaraswamy, played a prominent part in public affairs. He was the first Tamil-speaking member of the Ceylon Legislative Council. Ananda's father, Muthu Coomaraswamy, was born in 1834. He was educated at the Royal College, Colombo, and at the early age of seventeen got the much-coveted Turnour Prize for proficiency in Greek, Latin, and English classics. He started legal practice five years tater, and in 1856 he was appointed to his father's seat on the Legislative Council. The following year he was called to the bar at Lincoln's Inn in England. Later he was knighted by Queen Victoria.[3] Judging from his portrait, Sir Muthu must have possessed a very impressive personality. We see a robust man, dressed in a dark coat buttoned to the neck, dignified in expression, with a curling moustache, a well-groomed beard and piercing black eyes. Sir Muthu was associated with many scientific and cultural bodies in England as well as Shri Lankā. But his real interests were literary and religious. He translated from the Pali two Buddhist texts: the *Dāthavamsa,* a history of the sacred tooth relic of the Buddha which is believed to be enshrined in a *stūpa* at the ancient city of Polonnaruva, and the *Sutta Nipāta,* in which some of the discourses of the Buddha are recorded. He also translated an old Tamil play and published the English version under the title of *Arichandra, The Martyr of Truth.* The theme is taken from the *Ramayana,* but the play has a strong Buddhistic flavor.

In 1875 Sir Muthu Coomaraswamy married an English lady, Elizabeth Clay Beeby. The bride adapted herself very well to her new home in Shri Lankā, so different from her native land. She was delighted with the tropical beauty of the country and tried to understand the life and culture of its people. About two years after the marriage — on August 22, 1877, to be precise — Sir Muthu and Lady Coomaraswamy were blessed with a son. They named him Ananda, after the Buddha's favorite disciple.[4] As his mother's family home was in Kent, Ananda also got the somewhat unusual middle name, Kentish. When the child was barely two years old, his parents decided to take him to England. Mother and son commenced their journey, and Ananda's father was supposed to follow a month later. But the very day he was scheduled to sail, Sir Muthu suddenly died at the age of forty-six.

Ananda was brought up by his mother, whom he always held in the highest esteem. She must indeed have been a woman of remarkable courage and intelligence. Widowed at thirty, she never remarried. She led a quiet, studious life in England. She read all the journals in which her famous son's writings were published. Although she had spent only a brief period in Shri Lankā, her observation and reading had convinced her that the cultural roots of her husband's motherland lay in India. She impressed upon Ananda the need for a deeper understanding of the ancient philosophical and religious tradition of India. On her death in 1939 Ananda Coomaraswamy said, "I hope that by my efforts and work I have done something to help in the realisation of her desire."

II *Childhood and Youth*

Ananda was admitted to Wycliffe School in Springfield, England, at the age of twelve.[5] He did consistently well at school, not only in his studies but also in sports and other outdoor activities, and passed the matriculation examination at the earliest permissible age. In 1897 he paid a brief visit to Shri Lankā and

attended to some matters relating to his father's estates. On his
return to England, he joined the University College. Meanwhile he
had already written a number of essays on varied themes. One of
these was on the geology of the area surrounding Wycliffe School;
another was a defense of vegetarianism. During his first two years
at University College he won several prizes for his scientific studies
and would have won many more had the minimum age requirement
not disqualified him. In 1900 he secured the bachelor of science
degree with First Class honors in Geology and Botany. Three years
later he was appointed director of a survey of the mineral resources
of Shri Lankā. He went to his native land and performed his official duties with outstanding success while working for his Doctor of
Science degree. The doctorate was awarded to him on the basis of
his research papers, which he submitted under the title *Contributions to the Geology of Ceylon.*[6]

It might appear from the above account of Ananda's career as a
student that his interests lay almost exclusively in the field of the
natural sciences. But such was not the case. He had inherited his
father's catholic tastes, and even in his boyhood he pondered
deeply over his mother's estimate of the far-reaching significance
of Indian thought and culture. He read books on history, art,
philosophy, religion, and mythology. His flair for languages
enabled him to attain proficiency in Latin, Greek, French and
German. His extraordinary command of English is revealed in his
frequent and apt allusions to passages from the English classics.
Even his earliest writings show the ease, felicity and precision with
which he could handle English prose. His thorough grounding in
Western culture, combined with his innate love for and insight into
the Eastern — particularly the Indian — tradition, enabled Coomaraswamy to return to his motherland with an unusually rich
equipment.

III   *Four Years in Shri Lankā*

Coomaraswamy took his scientific assignment very seriously. He
gave several learned addresses on the geology of Shri Lankā. One
of these was given at Colombo museum. He is also credited with
the discovery of a radioactive crystal which was given the name
thorianite. It soon became apparent, however, that he was not a
specialist by temperament and that his scientific researches were
not enough to channel his intellectual energy. He plunged into the

study of Hindu and Buddhist texts. This effort demanded a thorough knowledge of Sanskrit and Pali, which he acquired in a remarkably brief period. He also participated in the social, cultural, and educational life of his country. He was the moving spirit behind the foundation of the Ceylon Reform Society and the publication of the Ceylon *National Review.* In these and other endeavors he had the support of his cousins, Sir Ramanathan Ponnambalam and Sir Arunachalam Ponnambalam. Apart from his interest in the life and culture of the Sinhalese people as a whole, Coomaraswamy gave special attention to the distinctive role of the Tamil-speaking community.

These years in Shri Lankā brought home to Coomaraswamy the negative side of the impact of the West on Asian countries. His geological researches took him to the villages, where he saw the devastating effect which modern industry was having on the traditional handicrafts. He was saddened not only by the economic ruination of the indigenous craftsman but even more by the corruption of his taste and the steady deterioration in the quality of his products. In the cities he saw how Western education was destroying the unity of the traditional life-style which had, through all the vicissitudes of history, preserved a harmonious and satisfying set of values. These observations gradually led him to a deeper study of cultural issues in general and of traditional arts and crafts in particular.

IV *Studies and Travels in India*

Coomaraswamy completed his work in Shri Lankā in 1906. During the next ten years he travelled extensively in India, though he returned to England again and again. His first journey in India was undertaken in December, 1906. On this trip he stayed for only three months, visiting archaeological sites, studying at libraries and museums, meeting people of divergent persuasions. He tried to delve deep into the foundations of India's five-thousand-years-old cultural history and saw the innate vitality of a tradition which appeared, on the surface, to be in a state of stagnation. He also saw signs of a new pride in India's ancient culture and tried to understand the new trends through which Indian nationalism was expressing itself. Among those who were working for a revival of interest in India's spiritual heritage, the Theosophists occupied an important place.[7] Although the Theosophical Society did not reach out to the masses, it exercised considerable influence among the intellectuals. Coomaraswamy came in close contact with the Theosophists and met Mrs. Besant several times. Whether or not he actually became a member of the Theosophical Society is a question on which accurate information is not available.

Three years later Coomaraswamy came to India again for a longer visit. By this time his interest in Indian culture had crystallized into a special knowledge of (and feeling for) Indian art. He had also made friends with some outstanding exponents of Indian art, philosophy, and religion. Among these were Rabindranath Tagore and his nephews, Abanindranath and Gaganendranath, the founders of the Bengal School of Indian painting.[8] Coomaraswamy spent several days at Calcutta as a guest of the poet. This was the beginning of a lifelong friendship. Long before the award of the Nobel Prize brought fame to Rabindranath Tagore, Coomaraswamy had grasped the deep significance of the poet's work. He always felt closer to Tagore than to Gandhi, although the latter probably represented the orthodox tradition — which Coomaraswamy accepted — more directly than the poet did. But, as his essays bear out, he did not indulge in uncritical glorification, whether of Rabindranath's poetry, music, and painting or of the work of Abanindranath and his followers.

Coomaraswamy delivered lectures at the invitation of The National Council of Education and the Indian Society of Oriental Art. One of these meetings was presided over by Swami Vivekananda's American disciple, Margaret Noble, who had adopted the Indian name, Nivedita. Later, Coomaraswamy and Sister Nivedita became good friends and collaborated on a book on the mythology of the Hindus and the Buddhists. After the conclusion of his stay at Calcutta, Coomaraswamy travelled extensively throughout northern India. It was during this tour that he collected the valuable sculptures and paintings which later became the nucleus of the Indian section of the Boston Museum.[9] He brought to light many forgotten aspects of Indian art and pointed out the true value of paintings and sculptures whose significance had remained unnoticed. To mention only one example, Coomaraswamy was the first to grasp the importance of the Pahari school of medieval painting which had been either ignored by art critics or regarded merely as a minor branch of the Rajput school. In 1911 he was placed in charge of the Art Section at the United Provinces Exhibition at Allahabad. He read a paper on *Swadeshi, True and False,* in which he stressed the need of protecting India's handicrafts from the onslaught of Western industrialism.

A few months later Coomaraswamy visited Kashmir and the Punjab. He continued his study of Indian painting and collected specimens of the Pahari style as developed in the Jammu region. He also collected some Panjabi folk-songs and studied the meanings of these songs in the light of the religious feelings which the melodies expressed. The following year he again visited Bengal and spent a few days at the school which Rabindranath Tagore had established at Shantiniketan. Coomaraswamy expressed his agreement with the poet's educational ideals and described the foundation of Shantiniketan as an important event in the cultural history of modern India.

V *Life in England*

In 1906 when Coomaraswamy returned to England after his long visit to Ceylon and his three months' tour of India, his basic philosophy of life had already taken shape. He had become convinced that the dichotomy between art and craft, between beauty and utility, between religion and life, was the darkest feature of modern civilization. This conviction naturally led him to seek out kindred spirits who shared his apprehensions about the mechanization of life resulting from the growth of technology. His circle of friends in England included those who wanted to go back to the countryside and who showed their concern for the traditional values by adopting a simple and harmonious pattern of life. Two names are particularly worthy of note: C. R. Ashbee and Eric Gill. The first, an architect by training, was influenced by the writings of Ruskin and William Morris. Like Coomaraswamy, Ashbee was deeply disturbed by the increasing threat which large-scale industry posed for handicrafts. He became a leader of the Arts and Crafts Movement and founded a workshop called the Guild of Handicraft.[10] In 1902 the workshop was moved to a small town called Chipping Campden, Gloucestershire. Ashbee's interests were many. Under his leadership about seventy workmen produced metalware, traditional jewelry and furniture. A small press was also established for printing books and pamphlets on the arts and crafts.

Coomaraswamy's wife, Ethel, had a brother, Fred Partridge, who joined Ashbee's workshop as a silversmith. Fred introduced his sister and her husband to his friends at Campden. The idealism of Ashbee and his associates and the congenial atmosphere of this quiet town so impressed Coomaraswamy that in 1907 he purchased an old house called Norman Chapel, not far from the workshop. The Coomaraswamys and the Ashbees became close friends. They had long walks together in the countryside and exchanged ideas on a variety of subjects. Their backgrounds were very different, but their philosophies of life converged on many points. Many years later Ashbee wrote in his journal, "It is on the anti-industrial side that he and I are so near to one another. I have always felt in him a profound understanding of what I am aiming at."[11] During his stay at Campden, Coomaraswamy published his first important work, *Medieval Sinhalese Art,* and several shorter works, including *The Aims of Indian Art* and *The Influence of Greek on Indian Art.* In 1910 Coomaraswamy left for India on a long visit; Ethel stayed behind. They intended to make Norman Chapel their permanent home, with frequent journeys to India and Shri Lankā. It soon became apparent, however, that Ananda was becoming more and more deeply involved with India. He decided to settle down at Banaras and dedicate his entire life to the study and interpretation of Indian culture. The connection with Campden was given up, much to the regret of the entire community. As it turned out, the idea of settling down at Banaras also did not materialize.

Coomaraswamy was introduced to Eric Gill by a common friend, William Rothenstein, who was himself an enthusiastic student of Indian art and poetry. Unlike many other admirers of Indian culture, whose interest in India was primarily aesthetic, Eric Gill brought to his study of art a deeply religious and philosophical temper. That is why Coomaraswamy felt closer to him than to other English friends although personal contacts between the two were few.[12] During their conversations they discovered a remarkable identity of convictions on fundamental matters, though Coomaraswamy's spiritual roots lay in the teachings of the Upanishads while Eric Gill found his inspiration in Catholicism. The two scholars collaborated with each other in many ways and continued a regular correspondence even after Coomaraswamy moved to America. In his *Autobiography,* Eric Gill has paid a tribute of admiration and gratitude to Coomaraswamy. He illustrated many of Coomaraswamy's writings with beautiful line drawings and also made a wood-engraving which served as a monogram for Coomaraswamy's personal library.

Although the major portion of Coomaraswamy's time in

England was spent at his secluded home in the countryside, he took an active interest in Indian affairs and accepted many speaking engagements in London. He became Associate Editor of *Isis,* a journal devoted to the study of Indian civilization. He was in touch with prominent scholars in such varied branches of Indology as art, music, religious movements, and archaeology. He followed with great interest the latest developments in palaeography, philology and field-archaeology with special reference to India. Nor were his activities confined to academic work. He identified himself with the nationalist movement and spoke up in defense of every struggle against injustice and oppression. In 1914, when Gandhiji (who had not yet become the "Mahatma" in the eyes of Indians) came to London after his famous struggle against racism in South Africa, Coomaraswamy was one of the main speakers at a meeting where rich tributes were paid to the non-violent warrior.

VI   *The Boston Museum of Fine Arts*

In the course of his travels in India, Coomaraswamy had acquired a valuable collection of paintings and sculptures spanning a period of many centuries and representing a wide variety of styles and schools. He offered the entire collection to the Government of India for the establishment of a National Museum at Banaras. The offer was turned down. Coomaraswamy wanted to make Banaras his home so that he might be near his art collection and live in a city where the continuity of the Indian tradition had been maintained uninterrupted for millenia. The Government's rejection of his proposal compelled him to give up this idea. He was pondering about the future pattern of his work when an unexpected opportunity came his way. Professor Denman Ross of Harvard University, who was deeply interested in oriental art, invited him to Boston.[13] Coomaraswamy had met Professor Ross at meetings of the India Society in London, and the American scholar had been impressed by the Indian's erudition and sincerity. Having heard of Coomaraswamy's failure to interest the Government of India in his art collection, Professor Ross persuaded the Trustees of the Boston Museum of Fine Arts to acquire it. A new department of Indian Art was founded, with the Ross-Coomaraswamy Collection as its nucleus. Coomaraswamy was invited to take charge as the Keeper of the new department. His appointment was officially announced in the *Bulletin* of the Museum in its issue of August, 1917.

Boston became Coomaraswamy's home for the remainder of his life. For thirty years he toiled without respite, collecting, sorting out, and interpreting enormous quantities of research material on all aspects of the oriental tradition in general and of the Indian expressions of that tradition in particular. He performed his official duties conscientiously and with meticulous care. Within a few years of his appointment the Boston Museum possessed the finest collection of Indian art in America and one of the finest in the world. In 1922, Coomaraswamy was entrusted with the section on Mohammedan Art in addition to the Indian. In 1933 his official title was changed. Instead of being the Keeper of Indian and Mohammedan Art he was now Fellow for Research in Indian, Persian, and Mohammedan Art and remained in that position up to August, 1947. Many of his writings were originally published in the Bulletin of the Boston Museum. He also gave several public lectures under the auspices of the Museum.

But Coomaraswamy was by no means a recluse. He did not shut himself up in his office. He traveled extensively in India, South East Asia, and the Far East. His visit to Java and Cambodia in 1920 was particularly significant, as can be seen in his epoch-making work, *A History of Indian and Indonesian Art.* He also traveled inside the United States, lecturing at Museums and Universities. In 1924 he became the founder and first President of the India Culture Center at New York, and he was the first President of the National Committee for India's Freedom established at Washington in 1938. He took a prominent part in the activities of the East and West Association, which was formed in New York in 1941 with Pearl Buck as President. And, though geographically far removed from India and Ceylon, he gave close and continuous attention to developments in those countries. An important part of his work consisted of his worldwide correspondence with scholars, creative artists, and thinkers, and the guidance given by him orally to hundreds of researchers, some of whom came to Boston from distant countries to seek his advice. The extent of the influence which Coomaraswamy exercized in this way was not fully realized in his lifetime.

VII   *Last Days*

On August 15, 1947, India became an independent nation. In honor of the occasion Ananda Coomaraswamy addressed Indian students at Harvard and unfurled the flags of free India and Pakistan. He explained the symbolism of the Indian emblems, paid a tribute to Mahatma Gandhi, and expressed his conviction that the future of the whole world would depend upon the manner in which India utilized her freedom in the ages to come.[14]

A week later Coomaraswamy's seventieth birthday was celebrated all over the world. At a farewell dinner at the Harvard Club he outlined his plans for the future. He was usually extremely reticent about his personal life and rarely expressed his feelings in a sentimental manner. But that day, as he was taking leave of his friends and of the surroundings in which the major part of his adult life had been spent, he was overcome by emotion. "This is my seventieth birthday," he said, "and my opportunity to say Farewell. For this is our plan, mine and my wife's: to return to India next year, thinking of this as an *astam gamana,* 'going home.' There we expect to rejoin our son, Rama, who ... is now at the Gurukul Kangri learning Sanskrit and Hindi with the very man with whom my wife was studying there twelve years ago.[15] We will remain in India, now a free country, for the rest of our lives." Then, striking an even more intimate note, he said, "I have not remained untouched by the religious philosophies I have studied, and to which I was led by way of the history of art. *Intellige ut credas!* In my case, at least, understanding has involved belief; and for me the time has come to exchange the active for a more contemplative life in which it would be my hope to experience more immediately at least a part of the truth of which my understanding has so far been predominantly logical."[16]

Unfortunately Coomaraswamy was not destined to spend his last days in India. Only seventeen days after he made his farewell speech, he was struck down by a heart attack in the garden of his home at Needham, Massachusetts. His wife and one of his students, who were by his side when he collapsed, tried to revive him.[17] But he never regained consciousness. His death was mourned all over the world, and obituary notices were published by leading journals and newspapers. Eight years later, the ashes of Ananda Coomaraswamy were immersed in the Ganges at Allahabad.[18]

VIII *Private Life*

When one considers his enormous influence as a lecturer and a writer, surprisingly little is known about Ananda Coomaraswamy's personal life. This lack of information is primarily the result of his own reticence. He shunned publicity. One of the persistent features of the oriental tradition, which he accepted wholeheartedly, is the preference for anonymity. When some one suggested that he should write an autobiography, he said, "I have neither the disposition nor the time or interest for such a thing. What is more, it would be entirely anti-traditional, altogether against the grain.... It would be *asvargya,* 'against heaven.' "[19] However, a vivid portrait of Coomaraswamy the man emerges from the reminiscences of his wife, Dona Luisa, and the descriptions given by his friends, pupils, and admirers. In recent years, a good deal of valuable biographical material about Coomaraswamy has been collected by Shri Durai Raja Singam of Malaysia.[20] But some of the books published by Shri Singam are out of print; and the most important one, a volume of tributes published in 1974 under the title *Remembering and Remembering Again and Again,* was released in an edition limited to 825 copies and is not easily available. Out of respect for Coomaraswamy's desire for privacy, and without delving too deeply into the details of his domestic life, I shall merely attempt a brief outline of the human side of the man.

In order to get a clear idea of his day-to-day life we should concentrate on his years at Boston. Indeed the first fifty-five years of his life seem to be like a period of many-sided preparation for the last decade and a half.[21] After living near the Museum for several years Coomaraswamy bought a house on Beacon Street in downtown Boston. His schedule was rigorous and well regulated, interrupted only by a brief annual vacation in Maine and lecture engagements outside Boston. He rose at five in the morning and put in several hours of work before going to the Museum. He disliked driving, and his wife Dona Luisa drove him over to the Museum and brought him back. They did little entertaining in the conventional sense. Coomaraswamy's small social circle consisted of a few colleagues, pupils, and fellow-scholars. Later, when he moved to Needham, he sometimes invited friends for dinner. The house at Needham was a large one, something like a small museum in itself. Every room had beautiful things from distant parts of the world.[22] But there was no hint of ostentation or display in the arrangement.

His diversions were simple. He enjoyed Negro music and American folk music, though he always turned to Indian classical music when he felt the need of a deeper and more sublime stimulus. He preferred vegetarian food and had inherited from his Sinhalese ancestors a taste for boiled rice, but he was not a faddist or a fanatic in diet. He loved animals, particularly dogs, and was very fond of his own dog, Toby. But his real hobby was gardening. He built a rock garden and spent much time tending his flowers and vegetables. His early training in botany and geology made him as knowledgeable as he was sensitive in his role of gardener. His special interest was in cacti.

One of Coomaraswamy's colleagues has written a graphic account of his office at the Boston Museum of Fine Arts where he spent eight hours every week day and often worked even on weekends.[23] The office, known as the Back Study, was located in one of the large, high rooms west of the main entrance. He sat with his back to the light. His papers were neatly arranged, and the desk-table at which he worked was a model of tidiness. Between the desk and the wall there was a small table for his typewriter. On one side there was another small desk for his immense worldwide correspondence. Thousands of postcards and packages arrived at or departed from that desk every week. The staff of the Museum saw to it that Coomaraswamy was left undisturbed. He found in this office a congenial place not only for study but also for calm reflection.

IX *Personality and Character*

The personal appearance of Coomaraswamy was arresting. He was not a man one might easily pass by without noticing. He was tall, broad-shouldered, "with a leonine head of hair and an ascetic face," as one of his friends described him.[24] Though spare of frame he had a strong constitution. His face, prematurely lined because of his tremendous exertions, was usually serious. But it was often lit by an engaging smile. He appeared distinguished, aristocratic in the finest sense of the term, irrespective of the activity in which he was engaged. He walked erect, with measured steps. His hands were large, and his work in the garden made them rugged and tanned. His hair grayed when he was in his fifties, and his attempts to grow a beard were not particularly successful. His dress reflected the refinement of his taste. His suits were beautifully tailored, made of fine fabrics in subdued shades. He wore a gold ring set with a star sapphire, "a link with Ceylon and geology." Altogether, his demeanor was dignified, somewhat aloof, but never cold or arrogant. He was not indifferent to the lighter side of life, but he had no use for anything — or any one — shallow or supercilious; and his earnestness was reflected in his features.

Ananda Coomaraswamy was a man of strong will. He was completely in possession of himself. Everything about him was authentic; there was no difference between the exterior image and the inner reality. Almost all those who came in contact with him became his admirers, many held him in reverence, and a few became his devotees. Even those who disagreed with him on fundamental questions did not doubt the absolute sincerity of his convictions and felt compelled to give careful attention to every word he wrote or uttered, even if they eventually rejected his views. It was impossible to associate anything petty or false with him. If he appeared distant and reserved at times, it was because he functioned at an intellectual and spiritual altitude which others could not always reach. From his early childhood he had been reflective, and he retained his love of solitude all his life. One of his classmates at Wycliffe School says that Ananda was a recluse even in his student days, when "he was often glimpsed flitting along the corridors and stairways like a transient and embarrassed apparition."[25]

The most striking feature of his character was his total absorption in his work. He gave his very best to every project that he took up. For almost half a century he toiled with singleminded devotion for the accomplishment of his chosen work: the exposition of a way of life which was once universal and which (in his judgment) had found its most profound expressions through Indian art, philosophy, poetry, and religion. His concentration was amazing. After an interruption, he could go back to his desk and resume the thread of his ideas with the ease of an ivory carver returning to his unfinished statuette. The high standards that he had set for himself and the immensity of the field he had made his own compelled him to use his time carefully. This practice gave the impression that he was inaccessible. But many of his students have reported that his initial reserve was only a precaution. He wanted to be sure that the person seeking his help was really in earnest about his work and was qualified to profit by his advice. Once he was satisfied on these points he became informal and gave generously of his time and energy. He encouraged younger scholars to publish their work and submit their researches to the only test that really mattered: the test of truth.

Coomaraswamy's stupendous intellectual energy was at the disposal of an unusually penetrating mind. Hard work alone would not have enabled him to attain such successes in so many fields had it not been for his quickness of grasp, his ability to distinguish the valuable from the secondary, his perception of relationships between ideas and events which many other scholars had missed. He was, in other words, not only sincere and industrious but also extremely competent. He had the knack of doing everything elegantly and skillfully. Since his main title to fame was his scholarly work in various fields of culture, his other talents remained unnoticed. For instance, very few among his admiring readers knew that he was also a painter and a poet. He illustrated many of his essays with his own drawings. He wielded the brush, the pen, and the pencil with considerable success in sketching architectural outlines with great liveliness. His independent pictures, marked by fluency and firmness of lines, were done mostly in the Rajput style. But he also tried his hand with washes and chiaroscuro in the Western manner. He was a keen calligraphist with a vibrant, distinctive handwriting of his own. His photographic work shows an imaginative approach to the ancient sites where most of his pictures were taken. He was able to capture the mood and flavor of antiquity. He was also a skilled printer; when he was in England he printed and bound his own books.

There was a strong poetic streak in Coomaraswamy's personality which was noticed not only by his friends but even by casual acquaintances. It was sometimes revealed unexpectedly in remarks about things or people. He was sensitive to the beauty of nature. In his descriptions of ancient monuments the relationship between man's handiwork and nature's unseen presence is conveyed with great power.

In a subsequent chapter I will discuss the poetic aspect of Coomaraswamy's writings. At this point I will merely point out that his poems, though few in number, show an unmistakable command over poetic idiom in French as well as English. Three of his poems were published, with charming illustrations by Eric Gill, and won the praise of his literary friends. Most of Coomaraswamy's poems are based on the central theme of love. In his lines, human love is seen as an aspect of the harmony which pervades the universe. The influence of the oriental poetic tradition, in which conjugal love is seen as a symbol of union with the Infinite, is clearly reflected in some of the poems. And some others — *From New England Woods,* for instance — reflect his deep awareness of the bond between human love and nature's rhythm.

X   *Summum Bonum*

In the foregoing paragraphs we have seen some glimpses of

Coomaraswamy the man. We have noted varied sides of his personality: his dedication to work, sincerity, sensitivity, generosity, intelligence, and penetrating insight. But our estimate would remain incomplete unless we remember that all his qualities and talents were integrated in a fundamentally spiritual temperament and outlook. He was a deeply religious man — religious in the finest sense of the term; a man whose self-assurance was mellowed by humility and reverence and whose intellectual eminence never made him oblivious of the Real which transcends the intellect. An avowed adherent of the orthodox Hindu tradition, he was moved to the very depths of his being by many of the utterances of the Buddha, Muhammed, and Jesus. The convergence of the major religions on certain basic truths was for him not just an intellectually deduced conclusion but a felt experience. He was concerned with *religion* which unites, not with *religions* which divide. To Ananda Coomaraswamy, religion was not the formal acceptance of a set of beliefs but the permeation of one's being by the "peace that passeth understanding."

Referring to the last fifteen years of Coomaraswamy's life, his wife Dona Luisa says, "These have been years of *tapasyā,* of uninterrupted penance." Indeed, the older he grew the closer he came to the *sthitaprajna,* the man of perfect equanimity described in the *Bhagavadgītā.* Outwardly, there was no letting up in his stupendous industry, no slowing down of his intellectual energy. But those who were close to him knew that the vision was turning inwards. Even his facial expression mirrored this self-absorption. "He appeared to me," said one of his friends after his death, "like a reincarnation of Lessing's Sage."[26] And recalling the fatal moment when he was struck down by a heart attack his wife remarked, "In death he looked like a *rishi* in marble."

Although Coomaraswamy will be remembered as one of the great scholars of the modern age, in his own eyes the function of erudition was purely instrumental. He looked upon it as a means by which one can equip oneself for the journey leading to the highest good, the *summum bonum.* He accepted the traditional view according to which the ultimate goal of all truth-seekers is the same, though they may approach it by different paths. The final destination is emancipation, and it can be approached only by cultivating a spirit of detachment. Towards the end of his life Coomaraswamy saw the goal quite clearly and was preparing himself for it. He had made up his mind to follow the *vānaprastha* ideal and had informed his friends that he and his wife would soon begin the final chapter of their lives in a quiet retreat near the Himalayas.[27] He visualized a life of utmost simplicity, spent in retirement. The following sentences, taken from a letter which Coomaraswamy wrote shortly before his death, give us an inkling into his innermost thoughts. "We are not going to India for our health!" he said in this letter. "This *astam gamana* is like the home-coming of the salmon to its source. Does the salmon consider the obstacles, or the distance of the trip, or the hazard of the leap from one waterfall to another?"[28]

CHAPTER 3

The Scholar and His Work

I N this chapter I will point out some of the striking qualities of Coomaraswamy's work as a serious writer whose researches and expositions have influenced the world of scholarship in the modern age. The intention is not to separate the scholar from the thinker but rather to gain familiarity with the range of his interests, his methods of approaching his subjects, and his distinctive style, so as to enhance our understanding of his ideas. Habits of thought are revealed in habits of communication. This is true not only of those who put forward original systems of ideas but also of those who — like Coomaraswamy — disclaim novelty and adopt the deceptively simple role of expounding a tradition.

I *Range and Output*

Even a glance at Coomaraswamy's work is enough to reveal the sheer volume of his output and the unusually wide spectrum of his interests. In 1937, on his sixtieth birthday, he remarked that he had enough material to keep him busy for another span of sixty years. A bibliography published in the journal *Ars Islamica* in 1942 lists 494 essays and books. The list does not include his letters, nor are separate references made to his famous "footnotes," which often became miniature essays in themselves. And many more works were produced during the five years he was destined to live after the publication of this bibliography. But even more astounding is the variety of the themes on which he wrote. In order to give the reader a clear idea of Coomaraswamy's range, I will place the subjects in a few major groups. This is a purely tentative classification. Almost all his writings deal with more than one specific subject. Essays on art are also essays on philosophy, religion, or even education. However, the group listing will serve our present purpose of viewing his work as a whole. It should be noted that a formidable list of subjects is not important in itself if we approach it quantitatively. Its value lies in the fact that it can show us how his ideas, traversing different regions and following different paths, converge in a world-view that is basically unitive.

In the first group we have writings on the history of civilization and various comparative studies. His main concern is with India and Shri Lankā. He removes misconceptions resulting from prejudice or inadequate knowedge, illumines the persistent trends in India's cultural evolution, and gives an estimate of India's contribution to human welfare. Essays on the general theme of East and West can also be placed in this group. The comparative studies embrace the fields of philosophy, religion, aesthetics, and the arts. There are, for instance, essays on Indian and Western epistemology; the relation between Greek and Indian art; pantheism, Indian and Platonic; Vedanta and the Western tradition; evolution of music in India and the West. The comparative method is also employed in some studies of Chinese and Middle Eastern thought and culture.

The second broad group comprises philosophical and religious themes. There are essays on the nature and function of philosophy, on time and eternity, creation and emanation. There are ethical essays (for instance on "man's last end" and the concept of "Dharma"); psychological essays ("Puppet Complex" and "Spiritual Paternity," to cite only two instances); studies of Western philosophers like Plotinus, Nietzsche, Meister Eckhart; and essays on religious doctrines (e.g., on rebirth, omniscience, transmigration). Coomaraswamy's full-length studies of Hinduism and Buddhism show his interest in the medieval and modern, no less than the ancient, developments in these religious traditions. To this group also belong essays on mythology, symbolism, and exegesis.

Another major group, perhaps the most important of all, consists of essays on archaeology, art and aesthetics. There are histories of Indian and Indonesian art and of medieval Sinhalese art; essays on architecture (for instance, "Vishvakarmā"), sculpture (e.g., on Indian bronzes, images with many arms, early Buddhist iconography), painting — especially Rajput and Mughal styles — music (on musicology as well as on the meanings of songs), and dance. The most significant (and controversial) of Coomaraswamy's writings in this group are his interpretations of oriental and medieval European doctrines of art and beauty, and of the relation between the arts and the crafts. We shall consider some of these in considerable detail in a later chapter. The archaeological studies deal mostly with sites in India and Shri Lankā. But there are innumerable cross references to archaeological researches in other parts of the world.

The literary group consists of etymological essays, studies of individual poets (e.g., Vidyapati, Keshavadasa, Tagore) and various writings on the drama and the theatre. As we shall see later, many of his religious and aesthetic studies are permeated by such a strong poetic flavor that they might well be placed in this group. Finally, it should be noted that Coomaraswamy was deeply concerned with social and educational questions, and many of his essays may be classed under the general heading of social sciences and folk culture. The nature of folklore and popular art; folk motifs in handicrafts and their regional variations; the place of art and religion in education; the religious basis of Indian society; the role of women in the oriental tradition; spiritual authority in the Indian theory of gobernment; the concept of nationalism, its possibilities and dangers — these are some of the topics on which he wrote stimulating essays.

In addition to these subjects, Coomaraswamy aslo wrote specialized pamphlets on printing, dyeing, paper-manufacture, mats, lacquer-work, dolls and carpets. In his early years he made valuable contributions to mineralogy and geology. And he also made translations from Sanskrit, Pali, Tamil, Hindi, Sinhalese and Persian — some of them in collaboration with other scholars. And at the time of his death there were eighteen unfinished manuscripts on his desk. But his most impressive achievement is that he was able to sustain the high level of his writing, both in profundity of ideas and in brilliance of expression, in spite of this tremendous output.

II   *Back to the Sources*

Having obtained a fair idea of the range of his scholarship, and having seen some of the starting points of his numerous journeys in the realm of human thought and creativity, we can now turn to some other distinctive features of Coomaraswamy's work. One quality which strikes all his readers, whether laymen or specialists, is its authenticity. We are constantly aware of the enormous preparation and persistent research behind every statement Coomaraswamy makes. There is no trace of casualness in his writing. He does not make assertions without supporting them with the unimpeachable authority of source material. Here and there we find him using secondary sources, but we can be sure that he does so only after checking them with the primary sources. It was his constant endeavor — to quote his own words — "to speak with mathematical precision ... without making any affirmations for which authority could not be cited by chapter and verse."[1] This, he claimed, was a characteristically Indian technique.

The sources are not necessarily limited to ancient texts. What matters to Coomaraswamy is not just the antiquity of a text but its representative and authoritative character. His studies of Hinduism take him not only to the Vedas, the Upanishads, the Puranas, the Epics and the texts of the classical "darshanas," but also to commentaries and interpretations of medieval writers. He looks upon the great medieval poet-saints as no less authoritative than the sages of the Upanishads or the unknown author of the *Bhāgavata*. Similarly, in his studies of Buddhism he draws upon the later Mahayana texts in Sanskrit no less than the earliest Pali texts. His Christian sources include Meister Eckhart, Bonaventura, and other medieval mystics in addition to the Gospels, Augustine, and Aquinas. His references to the Islamic tradition are based on a perceptive study of mystics like Ibn-al-Arabi and poets like Jalal-al-Din Rumi, in whose writings he finds the spirit of the Quran preserved more truthfully than in the expositions of many theologians.

This concern for authenticity led Coomaraswamy to his philological researches. His writings show familiarity with Sanskrit, Pali, several Indian languages, Latin, Greek, Hebrew, French, German, and Chinese. He did not learn these languages as a hobby, or for a display of erudition. His sole purpose was to examine the source material to ensure that his deductions about the various aspects of the tradition he was expounding were firmly grounded in the original texts. He often used words in a manner which showed that he was deliberately dissociating himself from the interpretations of contemporary scholars — interpretations which, in his judgment, were marred by faulty etymology. As employed by Coomaraswamy, many words were rescued from the derogatory suggestions that they evoke in ordinary usage. For instance, he used *reactionary* in the sense of "starting all over again," and *superstition* in the sense of "standing over." By thus adhering to the literal meaning, he was able to present certain concepts in a favorable light. His aim was not to provoke a controversy but merely to point out the distortions that had resulted from a neglect of original meanings. A curator of a museum, he points out, is one who "cares for" or preserves works of art — not one who exhibits or advertises them. A holiday is not a day of idle merrymaking but a "holy day," with a sanctity that should be respected through dedicated work. An ornament is an *attribute,* not a decorative frill added to an object. Inspiration is "divine influence," not a hunch or a brain-wave!

In order to convey the original meaning, Coomaraswamy sometimes puts a hyphen between two parts of a word: for instance, individual is written as *In*-dividual and personality as *persona*-lity. In both cases the italicized portion suggests the original connotation of the word: *In* points to inwardness, and *persona* to the element of "masking" originally attaching to the word but now forgotten in popular usage. The same desire to be consistent with etymology leads Coomaraswamy to render Sanskrit words into English in a manner which might appear unorthodox. He translates *deva* as "angel" instead of "God," *sahaja* as "cognate" instead of "simple," *Nirvana* as "De-spiration" instead of "Extinction." A striking example of Coomaraswamy's attitude to this question is provided by his contribution to the volume of essays prepared by Radhakrishnan as a tribute to Mahatma Gandhi on his seventieth birthday.[2] Instead of making vague remarks about Gandhiji's character and achievements, Coomaraswamy analyzes the meaning of the word "Mahātmā" and says that in *some* of its connotations the term can be properly applied to him. But as for the applicability of the term "in its full meaning," "that must ever remain a secret between himself and God." This is typical of Coomaraswamy's insistence on the accuate use of terms, even when he is paying homage to a particular individual on a particular occasion.

III *The Stylist*

Great scholars are not always fastidious about the literary aspect of their work. In Coomaraswamy's writings, however, we find a wonderful combination of matter and manner. He had a distinctive way of expressing himself. He evolved for each of his essays an idiom which conveyed not only his ideas but also the feelings which were evoked by the ideas. His writings are marked by an artistic restraint which often masks the feeling element. But his appeal is to the heart no less than the head. Actually, he writes in many different styles, though they all bear the imprint of a literary demeanor unmistakably his own. He usually employs a prose that is pithy and precise. In a memorial tribute one of Coomaraswamy's admirers said, "As in old pieces of rare craftsmanship, there is not a part in his sentences that could be taken out of its context without destroying the whole meaning ... All his essays are linked together like the pillars and girders of a beautifully constructed edifice."[3] And referring to the clarity of his expression another scholar says, "His pen is a precision instrument ... His compact, condensed prose often presents a forbidding mosaic on the printed page, challenging attention nonetheless because of its rigorous exactitude, like that of a mathematical demonstration."[4] In this matter, again, Coomaraswamy was following in the footsteps of his ancestors, the ancient sages, in whose highly compressed *sutras* we see the art of "putting an ocean in a pitcher."[5] He would have doubtless endorsed the Sanskrit proverb that "the pleasure of cutting down one syllable is equivalent to the pleasure afforded by the birth of a son."

Coomaraswamy was not, however, obsessed with brevity for its own sake. When the situation demanded, he found ample room for leisurely narration or description, and even for occasional digressions. For examples of his unhurried style one can turn to his description of the Renunciation episode in the life of the Buddha, or his account of Radha-Krishna legends in his essays on Rajput painting. If he could be terse and detached, he could also be fluent and persuasive. Indeed one of his critics has complained that the compelling power of Coomaraswamy's style sometimes results in the acceptance of his views by the reader who is somehow led to suspend his own judgment.[6] But on occasions we find in his writings a power which is far from being gentle or placid. In his denunciation of the devastating effects of Western technology — in its baser aspects — on the traditional life and culture of India and Ceylon, he adopts a pungent style. Here we occasionally see him in a satirical vein. But the satire is never unfair, it is never based on distortion. It is the result of righteous indignation and deep sorrow at the loss of something precious in the pattern of human living. Even the titles of some of his essays are ironical: for instance, "What Is the Use of Art, Anyway?"; "The Bugbear of Literacy"; "On Being in One's Right Mind."

As examples of this strong, even angry style the following may be cited. Of the so-called civilizing mission of Europe he says, "It can only be explained on the principle that misery loves company." As for the attempt of the Western rationalist to save unfortunate orientals from superstition, "it reminds us of the fox in the fable who lost his own tail and persuaded other foxes to cut off theirs." The collector of folk art is arraigned in these words: "The preservation of a people's art in folk museums is a funeral rite, for preservations are only necessary when the patients have already died."[7] On interpretations of Hinduism offered by some Western scholars we have this comment: "A faithful account of Hinduism might well be given in the form of a categorical denial of most of the statements that have been made about it, alike by European scholars and by Indians trained in modern modes of thought."[8] Westerners are by no means the only targets of Coomaraswamy's satire. Indians who aped the British and used nationalist sentiment for their own ends have also been dealt with sharply. "We have destroyed our industries and degraded the status of our artisans," he wrote. "And when at last our pockets were touched then, so far from realising what we had done, we set ourselves to form 'swadeshi' companies for making enamelled cuff-links (with pansies on them), for dyeing yarn (with German dyes), or for making uncomfortable furniture. We lived in caricatured English villas, and studied the latest fashions in ties and collars as we sat on the verandahs of Collectors' bungalows ... We learnt to adorn our walls with German oleographs and our floors with Brussels carpets, and then we thought of saving our souls by taking shares in some Swadeshi soap company."[9]

Unfortunately, passages like those quoted above were singled out from Coomaraswamy's writings by some of his reviewers. An inaccuate image was thus created. It should be remembered, however, that side by side with the detached, precise expositor and the wrathful critic there is a third Coomaraswamy: tender, sensitive, whose words convey the joy of existence and the principle of beauty which pervades the universe. Even his most scholarly essays contain memorable sentences that lighten the heavy weight of facts and hypotheses — sentences that could only be written by one who was truly a poet at heart. I will point to only two or three examples of Coomaraswamy's poetic style. In his essay on "Facial Expression in Indian Art"[10] he first describes the image of Sundaramūrti with its "breathless eagerness and rapturous surprise," and then the image of a Dhyāni Buddha, "lost in the passion of repose." In a few well-chosen words he evokes a contrast more vivid than any that could have been described by a learned iconographical analysis. Even more poetic is his description of "Night Effects" in Indian painting.[11] For the Indians, night is the time of discourse, entertainment, travel, worship, and love — "a time of exquisite contrasts when the torch of a guide or the flame of a camp-fire lights up the travellers' faces, or candles illumine the gold-inwoven dress and tinkling jewels of the dancer.... At night the lover waits for his beloved. At night the gods are borne in procession round the temple ambulatory with music and dance. And it is at night that men and women steal away to lonely hermitages to talk with those for whom the world is vanity, or go with offerings and devotion to some forest shrine of Mahādeva."

Here is Coomaraswamy's comment on a medieval Rajput miniature. After describing the atmosphere of "romantic loveliness," and the "delicacy and purity" of the artist's vision of a bride on her way to her husband's home, he says, "There is a haunting charm in the gentle shyness of the bride led to the bridal chamber. We can almost hear the wild beating of her heart and feel the tremulous touch of her red-stained fingers. We can see the marble building glistening in the moonlight. The whole picture bears the spell of that strange serenity and recollectedness that so distinguish the old life of India and survive so little in the life of non-rhythmic haste and hideousness into which it is so quickly changing."[12] Equally poetic, but more evocative of the sublime than of the beautiful, is his famous description of the dance of Shiva: "In the light of Brahma, Nature is inert, and cannot dance until Shiva wills it: He rises from his rapture, and dancing sends through inert matter pulsating waves of awakening sound, and lo! matter also dances appearing as a glory round about Him. Dancing, He sustains its manifold phenomena. In the fulness of time, still dancing, he destroys all forms and names by fire and gives new rest."[13]

It will be seen that by judicious use of alliteration ("He rises from his rapture"), and by the repetition of certain word endings in a single sentence (dancing, pulsating, awakening, appearing), an effect of rhythm and dynamism has been created. Other literary devices are used when he describes the same subject — the dance of Shiva — in the aspect of terror and power rather than of creativity and rhythm. In the following passage we see how Coomaraswamy uses archaisms and inversions in order to preserve the impression of awe-inspiring power in the ancient myth which he retells:

Shiva appeared in disguise amongst a congregation of a thousand sages and in the course of disputation confuted them, and so angered them thereby that they endeavoured by incantations to destroy him. A fierce tiger was created in sacrificial flames and it rushed upon him, but smiling gently he seized it with his sacred hands, and with the nail of his little finger stripped it of its skin, which he wrapped about himself.... The sages renewed their offerings and produced a monstrous serpent, which Shiva seized and wreathed about his neck. Then he began to dance. But there rushed upon him a last monster in the shape of a hideous, malignant dwarf. Upon him the God pressed the tip of his foot, and broke the creature's back so that it writhed upon the ground; and so with his last foe prostrate Shiva resumed the dance, of which the gods were witnesses.

Ordinarily, we would not find Coomaraswamy using constructions like "upon him the God pressed the tip of his foot" or "so angered them thereby that they endeavoured by incantations to destroy him." But he does not hesitate to take such liberties with idiom when they help convey the flavor of antiquity.

IV *Works: The Early Phase*

The remainder of this chapter will be devoted to a brief survey of Coomaraswamy's works in chronological order. The purpose is to see how his interests developed and to note the shifts of emphasis within the framework of a single world view. I will distinguish three main phases of his career and will give an outline of the important works of each phase. However, works to be discussed more fully in subsequent chapters will merely be pointed out at this stage, the contents and the main arguments indicated without detail. For further information regarding dates and names of publishers, the reader is referred to the bibliography at the end of this volume.

Coomaraswamy's earliest writings were connected with his professional work as a geologist. His researches were incorporated in his report to the Mineralogical Survey of Ceylon. By the year 1907, however, his interest had definitely shifted to the study of the arts and handicrafts of Ceylon, and then of India. He also became deeply involved in the cultural side of the nationalist movement. These concerns are clearly reflected in the important works of his early phase, which may be assigned roughly to the period from 1907 to 1917. *Medieval Sinhalese Art* (1908) may be described as Coomaraswamy's first major work. It soon established itself as the standard book on the subject. The author shows a remarkable sense of discrimination and a fine feel for the fundamentals of oriental art, particularly sculpture. Other essays on sculpture written in this period are *Ceylon Bronzes* and *Mahayana Buddhist Images from India and Ceylon*. We do not see in these early art studies the metaphysical insight which characterizes Coomaraswamy's maturer works. But there is already much evidence of synthetic power, enabling him to see the arts in relationship to other aspects of culture: religion, mythology, poetry, music. An essay on Vidyapati and another on Punjabi and Kashmiri songs indicate an interest in medieval culture. The essays on *Indian Craftsmen* and *The Arts and Crafts of India and Ceylon* show that his basic convictions regarding the true place of art in human life had already been formed.

Some of Coomaraswamy's early essays were published in the volume *Art and Swadeshi* (1910). This is an important work showing that even at this early stage of his career Coomaraswamy's concern about the arts and crafts of India and Ceylon was only a part of his general concern for that unified tradition which was being threatened by the cultural, political, and economic aggression of the West. Some of the essays, for instance *Svadeshi: True and False, Art and Swadeshi, Education in Ceylon*, and *The Function of Art Schools in India,* point to an interpretation of nationalism in terms of spiritual, aesthetic, and educational values rather than in terms of the struggle for political power. Others, such as *Facial Expression in Indian Sculpture, Night Effects in Indian Pictures,* and *The Modern School of Indian Painting,* indicate a deepening knowledge of the technical side of art. The essay on Tagore's poetry is one of the earliest studies of the poet, written long before the award of the Nobel Prize brought him fame. The volume includes a lecture on Mughal and Rajput painting in which some of the author's views, elaborated later, are anticipated.

Four other works of this early period deserve mention. First, there is the delightful volume *Myths of the Hindus and the Buddhists* (1914), prepared in collaboration with Sister Nivedita. The stories have been retold beautifully and with a deep insight into symbolic meanings. This book has retained its popularity — justly so, because here we see how Indian mythology serves as a bridge between the abstract concepts of the philosopher and the religious attitudes and beliefs of the common man. Secondly, there is a brief but significant essay, *What Has India Contributed to Human Welfare* (1915), in which Coomaraswamy gives his first clear and forceful statement of the fundamentals of the Indian tradition. This essay was later included in the famous work, *Dance of Shiva.*

Thirdly, in *Buddha and the Gospel of Buddhism* (1916), we have a pioneering work in which many misconceptions about Buddhism are removed, and the continuity between Hinduism and Buddhism is brought out effectively. Several outstanding Indologists have stated that they were first drawn towards the study of Buddhism through this book.[14] Almost simultaneously with this study of Buddhism, Coomaraswamy published his *Rajput Painting* which soon became one of the classics of modern art-criticism. The book is important for three reasons: it presents much new material on hitherto neglected styles of the Rajput school, it demolishes the notion that Rajput painting was merely a branch of the Mughal school, and it places the work of Rajput painters in the main stream of Indian culture by emphasizing its spiritual content.

V *Years of Maturity*

Coomaraswamy's appointment as the Keeper of the Indian section at the Museum of Fine Arts at Boston marked a turning point in his life. His most solid and enduring contributions to scholarship, especially in the fields of art history and art-criticism, were made during the decade and a half beginning with his arrival at Boston in 1917. Even if he had done nothing else, the catalogues which he prepared for Boston Museum, and the portfolios of Indian art which he designed and edited, would have constituted a stupendous achievement. But in addition to this work he produced a monumental history of early Indian architecture in three volumes,[15] and one of the first serious accounts of early Indian iconography.[16] He wrote essays on specialized subjects: manuscript illustrations, terra cottas, textiles, shadowplays. He translated an important ancient text on classical dance — Nandikeshvara's *Abhinaya Darpana* — and published it under the title of *The Mirror of Gesture*. Some of the essays written during this period are marked by originality of interpretation, backed by a careful sifting of evidence. For instance, in *The Origin of the Buddha Image,* he demonstrated that, irrespective of the question as to where and by whom the first Buddha image was fashioned, the artists of the Mathura school were the first to transfer the concept of Perfection to a concrete human form. In *Mahāpralaya* he put forward some brilliant hypotheses regarding the motifs of the Primeval Flood and the Last Judgment in the mythologies of East and West. And in some essays of this period, for instance *The Mystery of Mahadeva,* there are indications of a shift to the metaphysical point of view. There are also a few notices of Chinese and Islamic art-works,[17] suggesting that Coomaraswamy was looking beyond India and Ceylon in his quest for a tradition which was once universal.

Three of Coomaraswamy's most important works during this period are *The Dance of Shiva* (1918), *History of Indian and Indonesian Art* (1927), and *Yakshas* (1928 and 1931). *The Dance of Shiva* bears the sub-title "Fourteen Indian Essays," though only twelve of them deal with themes connected with India. The remaining two are about Nietzsche and Shakespeare. In this slender volume of less than two hundred pages a variety of themes is taken up: aesthetics, Buddhist sculpture, Indian music, a medieval devotional sect (Sahaja). But running through them all there is a current of thought in which art mingles with philosophy and religion, and patriotism melts into humanism. Commending this book to Western readers, Romain Rolland says in his introduction to *The Dance of Shiva*, "I invite Europeans to taste the delight of this rhythmic philosophy, this deep, slow breath of thought. From it they would learn those virtues which, above all others, the soul of Europe needs today: tranquility, patience, hope, and unruffled joy — like a lamp in a windless place that does not flicker."[18]

The Dance of Shiva, perhaps his best known and most widely read book, shows Coomaraswamy's powers in their mature form. His approach is constructive. His tributes to Shakespeare and Nietzsche show how inaccurate is the notion that he is unfair to the cultural tradition of the West. He describes Nietzsche's teaching as "pure *nishkāma karma*" and says, "There exists a voluptuousness that is not sensuality, a passion for power that is not self-assertion, and a 'selfishness' that is more generous than any altruism. These are distinctions that Nietzsche himself is careful to insist upon, and only wilful misunderstanding ignores this."[19] As for those who consider Coomaraswamy a revivalist advocating a return to ancient or medieval times, they would do well to read the essay entitled *Young India*. Here, while he laments the loss of much that was beautiful and noble, he points his finger to the future, not to the past: "If for a moment it seemed that we desired to turn back the hands of the clock, that was only sentimentality, and it was not long before we remembered that fresh waters are ever flowing in upon us.... In India, as in Europe, the vestiges of ancient civilisation must be renounced: we are called from the past and must make our home in the future. But to understand, to endorse with passionate conviction, and to love what we have left behind us, is the only possible foundation for power.''[20]

History of Indian and Indonesian Art is the first systematic survey of the arts of the Indian subcontinent (including what is now Pakistan) and of South East Asia written by an oriental scholar. As the title itself suggests, Coomaraswamy looked upon the art of Java and other countries of that region as a continuation of a single tradition rooted in India. Although only Indonesia is mentioned in the title, Burma, Ceylon, Thailand, Cambodia, and Viet Nam are included in the survey. The work is wholly free from cultural chauvinism. The art of each country is studied in the context of its own national evolution. It is emphasized that although this art ''can only be understood in the light of Indian studies it derives its energy from indigenous sources.''[21] In conformity with his view that the fine arts and applied arts cannot be studied in isolation from each other, Coomaraswamy discusses — in addition to architecture, sculpture, and painting — such skills as embroidery, lacquer-work, jewellery, basket-making, even puppets. In almost every chapter there are illuminating comments about the interpenetration of Hindu and Buddhist elements in this part of the world.

The sections on India and Ceylon are naturally handled with even greater self-assurance, since the writer speaks ''from within,'' as one who is himself a product of the tradition he expounds. He draws upon all available sources: literary, numismatic, geological, palaeographic, and archaeological. He assures us in the Preface that he has based his observations on personal visits to the museums and sites. The list of museums given at the beginning of the volume includes many in small towns in India and the countries of Europe and the Far East. Coomaraswamy even gives critical estimates of the catalogues of several museums, bestowing praise and blame with impartiality. Sometimes, in the light of subsequent reading or observation, he reverses his own judgments by adding footnotes. So thorough is his treatment of his subject that in his description of specific pieces of sculpture of the Gandhara school he even points out which part of the drapery is of Western origin!

This work is marked by sound judgment. On several important issues concerning Indian art-history — for instance, the origin and extent of the Indus Valley culture, the Dravidian element in Indian art, the respective contributions of Gandhara and Mathura schools in Buddhist sculpture, the status of the Pahari style of late-medieval painting, the symbolism of temple architecture —

Coomaraswamy's estimates have been generally verified by subsequent researches. But along with patient analysis and balanced, discriminating evaluations, the *History of Indian and Indonesian Art* also contains illuminating comparisons through which the author is able to communicate the fundamentals of two or more styles or movements in a few well-chosen sentences. On the basis of several specimens of Mughal and Rajput miniatures, which he discusses minutely, he describes the Mughal style as "academic, dramatic, objective and eclectic"; while the Rajput is "an *aristocratic folk art,* appealing to all classes alike, static, lyrical and inconceivable apart from the life it reflects." A Mughal painting is a miniature: "when enlarged, it becomes an easel picture." A Rajput painting is "basically a reduced wall-picture: when enlarged, it becomes a mural fresco." The Mughal artist uses soft tonalities and atmospheric effects; the Rajput's colors suggest enamel or stained glass: colors are used to establish planes, not blended to produce effects. In Mughal art, the outline is precise and patient; in Rajput art, the outline is "interrupted and allusive, or fluent and definitive, but always swift and facile."[22]

Yakshas, published in two volumes (1928 and 1931), is a most impressive work of this phase as an example of specialized research. Once again we have a combination of acute philosophical and psychological perception with an enormous amount of information about a specific theme in Indian folklore, mythology, and art. The first volume opens with an introductory statement of the place of worship in Hinduism as preparatory to the goal of liberation. Coomaraswamy then discusses the meaning of the word *Yaksha:* originally "a wondrous thing or being," later "a sylvan deity"; the qualities associated with the concept of *Yakshatva* ("Yaksha-essence"); the different forms in which the Yaksha is conceived; Yaksha figures outside India, particularly in Japan; their various female counterparts (*Yakshinīs*); the description of Yakshas and Yakshinīs in Buddhist and Jaina texts; and the relation of the semi-divine Yakshas with the divine beings (gods), particularly Kubera. The third section contains details of Yakshas as tutelary deities, patron saints and guardian angels. Tibetan sources are examined, and the Yaksha concept is reassessed with reference to the beliefs of several tribal people. In the fourth section there is a discussion of shrines and temples — both Hindu and Buddhist — in which Yakshas are either worshipped or are otherwise accommodated. Special attention is given to the tree-and-altar motif and its importance in the evolution of Indian religious architecture; in the fifth section the modes of worship in Yaksha shrines are explained; in the sixth Coomaraswamy interprets Yaksha worship to make the important point that the so-called "Bhakti movement" was not an isolated sectarian trend (as many historians of Indian culture have asserted) but was deeply rooted in a theism which goes as far back as the first century B.C. The seventh section is devoted to the relation between Yakshas and Bodhisattvas, and the Yaksha elements in Buddhist iconography. The eighth and last section deals with the "Woman-and-Tree motif" which has played such an important role in Indian sculpture.

In Part II of *Yakshas* Coomaraswamy gives, in no less than forty notes, additional information about the topics raised in Part I, advances alternative theories and hypotheses, and offers hints and suggestions for further research. He then goes on to examine, in considerable detail, related subjects such as Water Cosmology, the Grail Motif, the Makara (Crocodile) Motif, the Lotus, Vases of Plenty, Bowls on Figure Pedestals, and River Goddesses. All these themes are discussed comparatively, bringing out the surface similarities as well as differences of attitude between the Semitic-European and the Indian conceptions. Coomaraswamy derives from his researches on these questions conclusions that are of the utmost significance for the cultural history of India. He shows that the Yakshas control "not so much the waters as mere waters" but that essence (*rasa*) in the waters which is the same as in the sap of trees, with the elixir (*amrita*) of the gods, and with the seed in living beings. They represent the Life Cult which, closely related to the worship of the Great Mother, was the primitive religion of India.[23] He sees in the Yaksha motif yet another proof of the fruitful blend of Aryan and indigenous genius, and asserts that "primitive survivals in current faiths are signs of fulfilment rather than failure." He demonstrates the continuity of "racial psychology" in India and shows how, within the framework of the *Philosophia Perennis,* an important place was found for popular religion at the practical level side by side with absolute monism at the transcendental level.

VI   *The Later Phase*

The essays which Coomaraswamy produced during the last phase of his life — roughly between the years 1934 and 1947 — reveal four distinct tendencies. In the first place, there is an increasing fascination with Vedic studies, as can be seen from the following titles: *Angel and Titan: An Essay in Vedic Ontology* (1935); *Vedic Exemplarism* (1936); *Vedic Monotheism* (1936); *Vedic Doctrine of Silence* (1937). His interest in the Vedas is primarily philosophical, not exegetical, though he often goes into the finer points of exegesis. Secondly, there is a reversion to the Western tradition in its medieval expressions, particularly in the field of art and aesthetics. Two volumes on *Medieval Aesthetics* (1935, 1938) belong to this period. There are interpretations of selected passages from Dante's *Paradiso,* essays on the Christian view of art, and a study of Meister Eckhart. Thirdly, we see a corresponding hardening of attitude towards modern Western "civilization." In many of the comparative essays of this period he shows close affinity between the oriental and the medieval Western traditions and a clear opposition between the oriental and the modern (industrial, technological) Western world-view. In essays like *Why Exhibit Works of Art?* and *Am I My Brother's Keeper?* there is sharp, often ironical, criticism of the modern West. Fourthly, we see a consistent attempt to apply the metaphysical assumptions of the Perennial Philosophy to social, political and educational problems. This can be seen in *The Religious Basis of the Forms of Indian Society* (1946) and *Spiritual Authority and Temporal Power in the Indian Theory of Government* (1942).

Though these tendencies led to certain shifts of emphasis they did not circumscribe Coomaraswamy's work in the slightest degree. Even in this last phase we see that incredible diversity and range of scholarship and that combination of specialized analysis with synoptic insight, which characterized his work of the preceding phase. Once again special problems in aesthetics are discussed and specific artworks examined with all the expertise that he possessed. But on closer examination even these specialized studies are seen to have been influenced by the author's metaphysical predilection. The same can be said of books on specific religious myths or ethical doctrines or specific aspects of folk culture. In all these studies one or more among the tendencies mentioned above are reflected, though this reflection is sometimes subtle and not apparent on the surface.

Representative examples of Coomaraswamy's work in this phase are *The Transformation of Nature in Art* (1934), *Why Exhibit Works of Art?* (1943), *Hinduism and Buddhism* (1943) and *The Bugbear of Literacy* (1944). The first among these deals entirely with art and aesthetics. It contains seven essays. One of these is on the medieval Christian view of art as represented by Meister Eckhart; the other six are on Indian themes, but they contain many comparative comments on Chinese, Islamic, and Christian concepts as well. In the very first essays, *The Theory of Art in Asia,* Coomaraswamy views the apparently divergent theories and attitudes in art in the context of a tradition which was shared by East and West. "There was a time," he says, "when Europe and Asia could and did understand each other very well. Asia has remained herself; but subsequent to the extroversion of the European consciousness and its preoccupation with surfaces, it has become more and more difficult for European minds to think in terms of unity, and therefore more difficult to understand the European point of view."[24]

Coomaraswamy opens his exposition with a clear statement of the fundamental aim of Indian art: the attainment of a condition in which "knower and known, seer and seen, meet in an act of transcending distinction." The corollaries of this objective are emphasis of concentration or immediate absorption (aesthetic intuition); the ideal determination of the forms of art; rejection of the distinction between "fine" and "decorative" art; and the synthesis of the pictorial and the formal, the outer and the inner, in a single criterion. He proceeds to discuss the question of criterion (*pramāna*) in greater detail and explains why oriental art steers clear of naturalism, in spite of the fact that it constantly expresses the universal rhythm which unites man with nature. The concept of *rasa* is then elucidated, and the differences between the Indian and the modern Western attitude are restated in the light of the positions discussed. Coomaraswamy draws part of his material from Chinese texts, particularly the *Six Canons of Hsieh Ho* and the *Chieh Tzu Yuan.* In his references to specific works of art he includes Japanese *Noh* plays and Chinese painting in addition to examples of Indian art. He also gives Chinese terms corresponding to Sanskrit words used in the ancient and medieval texts on aesthetics and poetics.

In the next essay he discusses Meister Eckhart's view that "art is a manner of speaking about God and Nature" and shows the close similarity between Indian and Christian conceptions of art. This presentation is followed by a discussion of the spectator's or the listener's point of view. The reactions to art are examined in terms of the responses of the expert, the devotee, the sophisticated man of taste, the scholar, and the average person. A brief chapter is devoted to the *Shukranītisāra,* a medieval work on aesthetics in which the criterion of beauty is stated specifically in relation to iconography. In the essay on *Paroksha,* the two viewpoints appropriate to the symbolic and the "obvious" are distinguished; while that on *Abhāsa* shows how the Indian artist's approach to the question of relief and perspective is influenced by the concept of "reflection" or "shining back" of the Infinite in the finite. The concluding essay, *The Origin and Use of Images in India,* explains the fundamentals of Indian iconography in the light of the concept of a personal God. The aesthetics of image-making is seen as determined by the psychological needs of the worshipper — needs which, it is stressed once again, are fully accepted in the Indian tradition in spite of the metaphysical postulate of the Impersonal Absolute. *The Transformation of Nature in Art* is, thus, one of Coomaraswamy's most important contributions. It is not an easy book to read, and that may be the reason why it is far less widely known than some of his other works.

Why Exhibit Works of Art? (later published under the title of *Christian and Oriental Philosophy of Art*) deals mostly with practical questions concerning the broad field of art creation and art appreciation. Only one brief essay, *Beauty and Truth,* may be described as theoretical. All the others show Coomaraswamy's deep apprehension that modern theories of art, with their emphasis on individual expression and glorification of "genius," might distort and ultimately annihilate the true place of art in human life. In *Is Art a Superstition or a Way of Life?* he gives an impassioned defense of the traditional evaluation of art as an inseparable aspect of the total harmony of life. *What is the Use of Art Anyway?* contains sharp criticism of the art historians and professors of aesthetics who "rejoice in the unintelligibility of art," which they "explain psychologically, thus substituting the study of the man himself for the study of the man's art."[25] In the concluding essay, *The Nature of Folklore and "Popular Art,"* he shows that the ancient Indian distinction between the universal and the local is not the same as the modern distinction between classic (or academic and supposedly important) and folk (secondary, superstitious and by implication of no abiding value). He points out the extremely important part which folk art is still playing in the preservation of a tradition threatened by modern commercialism.

Hinduism and Buddhism is a masterly presentation of the two

dominant traditions that have molded the lives of millions of people in the oriental world for at least twenty-five centuries. Almost
every aspect of Hindu and Buddhist philosophy, art, literature, and
mythology had been taken up by Coomaraswamy in his earlier
works. Now, in the closing phase of his career, he returned to his
theme with all his erudition and at the peak of his reflective powers.
This little book of seventy-four pages (and over three hundred
notes and references!) gives a highly condensed account of all that
is most fundamental for an understanding of the two faiths. Not a
line can be pruned without reducing the meaning-content. All the
controversial questions are taken up and answered succinctly in a
few sentences. Hinduism and Buddhism are dealt with in two separate essays, but their mutual relationship is always kept in view.

A statement of the positive features of Hinduism is preceded by a
removal of several misconceptions. Coomaraswamy points out that
the Vedic doctrine cannot be labelled either as pantheism or as
polytheism, and certainly not as Nature worship; that *Karma* is not
"fate" in the popular sense of the word; that *Māyā* is not "illusion"; that reincarnation is not "the return of deceased individuals
on this earth"; that the classical *darshanas* are not philosophical
systems but viewpoints, complementary rather than mutually
exclusive. He then goes on to explain the Vedic myth of the
primeval sacrifice and to establish the connection between the
Vedic gods (Agni and Indra) and their popular counterparts
(Krishna and Arjuna). Then comes the central argument of the
essay, in which the symbolism of the sacrifice is explained in terms
of the highest Reality in its aspects of unity as well as its manifestation in diversity. The Universal is seen in itself and also as it appears
in the individual. Theology coincides with autology, and "the only
possible answer to the question 'What am I?' must be 'That art
Thou' ... for as there are two Him, so there are, as all tradition
affirms unanimously, two in us; although not two of Him or two of
us, nor even one of Him and one of us, but only one of both."[26]
Some of the traditional metaphors through which this view of Reality is conveyed are then explained, with Coomaraswamy's customary literary competence.

The central symbol of the Sacrifice is next examined in terms of
practical activity: "the Sacrifice is something to be *done*."[27] In this
section Coomaraswamy gives a refreshingly new interpretation of
the famous *Karma-mārga*—Way of Works—of the *Bhagavadgīta*.
The Karma-marga, he says, is based on the conception of

Sacrifice as "an incessant operation." Every function of our active life, "down to our very breathing, eating, drinking and dalliance, is sacramentally interpreted." Hinduism thus "comes full circle." From the position that "the perfect celebration of sacrificial rites is our task" we come to the position that "the perfect performance of our tasks, whatever they might be, is itself the celebration of the rite." Thus understood, Sacrifice is no longer "a matter of doing specifically sacred things only on specific occasions, but of sacrificing (*making sacred*) all we do and all we are."[28] It is a matter of "the sanctification of whatever is done naturally, by a reduction of all activities to their principles." Finally, in the concluding section, the application of the basic principles to the Hindu social organization is examined. Thus the metaphysical, religious, ethical, and social aspects of the Hindu tradition are expounded in a logical progression and are also synoptically related with each other.

The study of Buddhism is marked by the same admirable combination of brevity and profundity. In some paragraphs there is unhurried attention to detail; in others, every sentence seems like the distillation of an idea so pregnant with meaning that in less competent hands than Coomaraswamy's an entire chapter would be required for explaining it. Once again he begins with the Myth. Rejecting the view of the historicists that the Buddha was "not Man but a man, subsequently deified," Coomaraswamy shows that the personality of the historical Buddha is completely overshadowed in its significance, "as he must have wished it should be," by the eternal substance with which he identified himself. The details of the Buddha's legendary life are then stated and the conclusion derived that "his birth and awakening are coeval with time."[29] The Myth is then connected with the Doctrine, in its metaphysical, psychological, ethical, and aesthetic aspects. The essay concludes with the demonstration that the Buddha is the Absolute. He *is* the Spirit (Atman), and Inner Man of all being; he is "That One" who makes himself manifold and in whom all beings again "become one."

Coomaraswamy's distinctive contribution to the understanding of Buddhism, as revealed in this brief essay, can be easily summarized. He shows the continuity between Hinduism and Buddhism, and even the identity of their approach on fundamentals. The notion that the Buddha rejected the Atman is shown to be the result of a complete misunderstanding of his references to the individual ego. The positive side of the concept of Nirvāna is pointed

out, as against the opinion generally held by Western scholars that
Nirvāna is annihilation or extinction of everything. The Buddhist
idea of rebirth is explained in conformity with the Vedantic view
that "there is transmigration, but there are no individual trans-
migrants." The Buddha of the Myth is interpreted as a solar deity,
like the Vedic Agni and Indra. And the Buddha-principle is identified with the Eternal Reality of which the scriptures of all religions
speak. "We are forced by the logic of the scriptures themselves,"
Coomaraswamy asserts, "to say that Agnendrau (Agni-Indra),
Buddha, Krishna, Moses, and Christ are names of one and the
same descent whose birth is eternal."[30]

   The Bugbear of Literacy is the title of a book published post-
humously (1949). It contains, besides the title essay, *Am I My
Brother's Keeper?, Paths That Lead to the Same Summit* and *East
And West*. There are also two anthropological studies — *Spiritual
Paternity* and *Puppet Complex* — and an essay on *Gradation, Evolution and Reincarnation*. In the title essay, Coomaraswamy makes
the points that there is no necessary connection between literacy
and culture; that the excessive importance now being attached to
formal literacy is the result of industrialization which "separates
wisdom from skills" and makes culture dependent on the ability to
read; and that the imposition of formal literacy upon a cultured but
illiterate people can be counterproductive. Coomaraswamy is
obviously not glorifying the lack of formal education. "My real
concern," he says, "is with the fallacy involved in the setting up of
'literacy' as a standard by which to measure the cultures of illiterate
people."[31] Blind faith in literacy tends to obscure the significance
of other skills. Addressing the Western educator, with his faith in
the magical power of the printed letter, he says, "You do not care
under what sub-human conditions a man may have to earn his
living if only he can read — no matter what."[32]

   Am I My Brother's Keeper? is a powerful indictment of the negative side of modern Western civilization. In the name of science this
civilization has brought to the peoples of Asia and Africa nothing
but confusion and exploitation. Its values are entirely commercial,
and it proceeds to "civilize" so-called backward societies by a constant multiplication of wants, destroying their sense of contentment
and shaking their faith in their own heritage. It preaches the gospel
of action as an end in itself, "while contemplation, the pre-
requisite of action, is disparaged as an escape from responsibility."
This inversion of values is only partly prompted by economic and

political interests. Behind this "proselytizing fury" there lies "a fanaticism which cannot accept any kind of wisdom that is not the product of pragmatic calculations."[33] Even the "goodness" of the modern world is unprincipled; even its "altruism" is "no longer founded on a knowledge of the Self, love of the Self, but on selfish calculation." How can the West atone for all the harm that it has done? Not by orientalizing itself, but "only by the recognition of the principles by which the East still lives." Coomaraswamy asks the European, for his own sake as much as for others' sakes, to "give up the cherished and flattering belief that he can do any good except by being good himself."[34]

Three other essays in this book deal with this broad theme. In *East and West* Coomaraswamy asserts that the conflict between East and West can be resolved only if the West understands the necessity of retracing its steps. Since it is the West which first abandoned the norms that were once common to the entire human civilization, the motion towards a rapprochement must originate in the West. "The primary problem is the reeducation of the Western literati," he says. Politicians and economists cannot clear the air. He adds, "Philosophers and scholars, to whom their knowledge of the Great Tradition has been a vital, transforming experience, can alone reach and verify the agreement."[35] Eulogizing the work of some Western scholars like Rene Guenon and Marco Pallis, he says, "Such is the leaven by which the epigonous and decaying civilisation of today can be 'renewed in knowledge.' " In *Eastern Wisdom and Western Knowledge,* special attention is given to Rene Guenon's work which many Western scholars find unpalatable because Guenon compels them to reexamine the foundations of their own culture. "Guenon does not ask Europeans to become Hindus or Buddhists but to rediscover Christianity — or rather, Plato," writes Coomaraswamy. But Coomaraswamy does not feel optimistic that men like Guenon will be heeded by Europeans in their present mood. "I often marvel at men's immunity to the *Apology,* the *Phaedo* and the seventh chapter of the *Republic.* I suppose it is because they simply would not hear, "even though one rose from the dead."[36] In *Paths That Lead to the Same Summit,* the criticism of the West is somewhat toned down, and the emphasis is placed on the ideas which were once shared by the East and the West. Coomaraswamy examines the reasons which led Christianity to abandon its earlier attitude of tolerance towards other faiths. He suggests that the excessive stress on ethics and the com-

parative neglect of the intellectual and aesthetic sides of man's
inner life might partly explain the self-righteous and intolerant attitude of post-Reformation Christianity. Referring to the evangelical
zeal of Christians, he comments, "The conversion we need is not
from one form of belief to another, but from unbelief to belief."
And again, "If you say: 'The light that is in you is darkness' you
are offending them and also the Father of all lights.... Never let us
approach another believer to ask him to become 'one of us,' but
approach him with respect as one who is already 'one of His.' "[37]

The purpose of *Spiritual Paternity* is methodological. In this
essay Coomaraswamy points out the erroneous approach of many
anthropologists to the study of primitive cultures. They look upon
primitive peoples in isolation from each other, assuming that their
ways of life are of local origin and have always remained static.
Coomaraswamy describes many of the beliefs of primitive communities as survivals of theories once held by sophisticated societies.
What we see is a common tradition in a state of fragmentation and
decline rather than unrelated and unchanging life patterns of men
who are too "savage" to understand the notion of progress. In
Puppet Complex Coomaraswamy gives a profoundly metaphysical
interpretation of the dance of the animated puppet. The Balinese
girl who moves like a doll dancing on a string is not reflecting any
"complex," as the anthropologist asserts, but is merely acting out
the ancient symbolism of human beings as "God's toys." The
dancer shows her obedience to one central cord rather than her sub-
jection to contrary, unregulated pulls, declares Coomaraswamy.
"If the puppets could speak the language of traditional philosophy,
they would say: 'It is not my self, that of these wooden parts, but
another Self — the Self of all puppets — that moves me. If I seem
to move of my own will, it is only to the extent that I have identified
myself, and all my being and willing, with the Puppeteer who made
me.' "[38] Without knowing it, the Balinese dancer, in her rapt ec-
stasy, is expounding though her gestures that Perennial Philosophy
according to which the All-Maker is the "Holder of Every
Thread." She is not "expressing herself," says Coomaraswamy,
but playing her part impersonally. "She is not the victim of a
'complex' but merely a perfect actress."

In *Gradation, Evolution and Reincarnation,* the concluding
essay in this volume, Coomaraswamy examines the alleged conflict
between the scientific concept of evolution and the religious doctrine of reincarnation. He shows that it is only with the animistic

notion of reincarnation that science can have any quarrel, not with the traditional doctrine. The former belief, popularly held, looks upon the individual ego as passing on from one embodiment to another. The latter accepts no other transmigrant than Ultimate Reality itself.

CHAPTER 4

Exposition of the Philosophia Perennis

A S we pass from the study of Coomaraswamy the man and the
scholar to a study of Coomaraswamy the thinker, one fact
must be clearly recognized at the outset. The ideas which he
expounds are not his own but those that he derives from a universal
and perennial body of doctrine which he accepts. In other words,
there is no such thing as the philosophy of Ananda Coomaraswamy. Throughout his career he disclaimed originality. A few
days before his death, in his reply to the tributes paid to him on his
seventieth birthday, he said, "I wish to tell you that I have added
nothing new."[1] Many years earlier he had asserted that he was "not
propounding views that I regard as my own, except in the sense that
I have made them my own."[2] In making these disclaimers he was
not just being modest. Nor was he evading the task of stating his
views clearly. Indeed, nothing can be clearer or more unadorned
than his statement of the views which he endorsed. "I should like to
emphasise," he said, "that I have never built up a philosophy of
my own, or wished to establish a new school of thought. Perhaps
the greatest thing I have learnt is never to think for myself. I fully
agree with André Gide that *toutes choses sont dites déjà,* and what I
have sought is to understand what has been said .... holding with
Heraclitus that the Word is common to all, and that Wisdom is to
know the Will whereby all things are steered."[3] Even in art criticism, a field in which he had such unrivalled expertise, he stated his
position in the same way: "These are not personal opinions but
logical deductions of a lifetime spent in handling art-works, of
observation of men at work, and the study of that universal philosophy of art from which our own 'aesthetic' is only a temporary
aberration."[4]

These disclaimers to originality must be accepted as sincere. Indeed they were so accepted by scholars who were very close to him. Referring to his lectures at Boston, one of his colleagues said, "With him a lecture no less than a book was a crystallization for the edification of others of certain elements drawn from the inexhaustible ocean of truth." And in the Preface to a Bibliography of Coomaraswamy's writings the editor says, "There are few scholars who ... have the ability and the courage to hand on a clear, uncompromising message of what they have seen, heard and learned. Never has he had time for, or interest in, presenting personal ideas or novel theories, so constantly and tirelessly has he devoted his energies to the rediscovery of the truth and the restating of the principles by which cultures rise and fall."[5]

I *"Thus Have I Heard"*

This disavowal of originality, this ascription of one's views to a hoary tradition, is itself an integral part of the tradition which Coomaraswamy expounds. In India, from remote antiquity right up to the modern age, rediscoverers have been instinctively respected; and those who claim to be discoverers have been suspected. The Vedic poet-sages, rightly regarded as the founders of a civilization which has retained its continuity for forty centuries, invariably refer to those who "saw" in bygone ages. "The Real is One: Seers have spoken of it in diverse ways." Anonymity is assumed to be the right attitude, individual expression is not encouraged. The *Prashna Upanishad* ends with the words: "Obeisance to the Great Seers!" So also does the *Mundaka Upanishad* conclude its teaching: "Hail to the Great Sages! Hail to the Illumined Souls!" We do not know the names of any of the artists who created the great masterpieces of Buddhist sculpture or painted the frescoes of Ajanta. Even Vyāsa and Vālmīki, to whom the *Mahābhārata* and the *Rāmāyana* are ascribed, are shadowy figures. So are the supposed founders of the classical philosophical systems. The wise man in the Indian tradition does not say to his disciple, "Verily, verily, *I* say unto thee." He prefers to say, "Thus have I heard, my son, from those who heard before me."

"The Buddha," says Coomaraswamy, "describes as a vile heresy the view that he is teaching a 'philosophy of his own,' thought out by himself. No true philosopher ever came to destroy but to fulfill the Law. 'I have seen,' the Buddha says, 'the ancient way, the Old

Road that was taken by the formerly All-Awakened, and that is the
path I follow.' ''[6] The teachings of the Sufi saints of medieval India
are imbued with the same spirit. And in our own age Mahatma
Gandhi, when praised by a Western admirer for contributing to the
modern world the doctrines of Truth and Non-violence, smiled and
said, ''I have contributed nothing. Truth and Non-violence are as
old as the Himalayas.''

Coomaraswamy has proclaimed his adherence to this view so frequently, and with so much emphasis, that we must accept the
genuineness of his desire to be regarded merely as the expositor of
an ancient tradition. His own distinctive contribution lies in his
comprehensive, lucid, and many-sided interpretation of that tradition and his attempt to apply it to the practical problems of the
world. It would be an exercise in futility to insist on seeking out
from his writings something which he declares repeatedly to be
nonexistent. Far more fruitful would be an inquiry into the meaning which he attaches to traditional wisdom. This inquiry would
include a study of the evidence he offers with regard to the perennial philosophy. It would also be useful to see to what extent his
interpretation is corroborated by those offered by some other outstanding thinkers of our age.

II   *A Universal Language*

As a result of a misunderstanding based on a onesided reading of
his works, Coomaraswamy is sometimes supposed to have
advanced the view that the perennial philosophy belongs exclusively to the East, or even to India. Actually, all that he claims is
that this philosophy has been *temporarily* eclipsed in the West but
still retains its vigor in the East. ''A philosophy identical with Plato
is still a living force in the East,'' he says.[7] There was a time when
the West shared that philosophy and when there was no basic conflict between Eastern and Western viewpoints. Referring to the
work of Rene Guenon, Coomaraswamy says, ''If Guenon wants
the West to turn to Eastern metaphysics, it is not because it is *Eastern* but because it is *metaphysics*.''[8] The West, he complains, ''in its
desperate attempt to live by bread alone,'' has turned away from
metaphysics. He adds, ''The contrast is not between East and West
as such but between those paths which the rest of mankind follows
as a matter of course and those post-renaissance paths that have
brought us to our present impasse.''[9]

The difference between the perennial and the transitory ("fashionable") types of philosophizing is not geographical but cultural. Coomaraswamy emphasizes that the Perennial Philosophy is based upon the "natural and ordinary" way of life, and its rejection is the inevitable outcome of the modern "irregular" way of life which the West has adopted and which it seeks to foist upon the rest of the world. But this need not be the situation in the future. If only the West reexamines its own cultural heritage it will discover the meeting ground between different cultures and ways of living, declares Coomaraswamy. "There is a universal language, verbal and visual, of the fundamental ideas on which the different civilizations are founded. In this commonly accepted axiology or body of first principles there is a common universe of discourse."[10] Different culture-styles (if we exclude the modern West) are like different dialects of this one language, expressing the same ideas "often through identical idioms."[11] The *philosophia perennis* can therefore, with equal justification, be described as *philosophia universalis*. And if it once helped mankind evolve a satisfying, harmonious way of ordering its affairs, practical as well as spiritual, there is no reason why it should be unable to do so again.

Using the same metaphor, he says in another context, "If we leave out the modernistic, individualistic philosophies of today, and consider only the greatest traditions of magnanimous philosophers, it will be found that distinctions of East and West are comparable only to differences of dialect, while the essential spiritual language remains the same."[12] East-West dichotomies have been artificially established on the basis of alleged divergences between the temperaments of men in the two hemispheres. "But the divergences of character are superficial", says Coomaraswamy, "and deeper we penetrate the more we discover an identity in the inner life of Europe and Asia. Can we, in fact, point to any elemental experience or any ultimate goal of man which is not equally European and Asiatic? Does one not see that these are the same for all ages and continents?"[13]

Not content with making these general statements of affinity, he points to specific thinkers, poets, and artists who exemplify the common tradition which once united East with West. Plato, Philo, Marcus Aurelius among the ancients; Saint Augustine, Saint Ambrose, Meister Eckhart among medieval thinkers; Nietzsche, Blake, and Walt Whitman in the modern age: these Westerners are in no way alien in their spirit to the most typical orientals. "Who

that has breathed the clear mountain air of the Upanishads, of
Gautama, Shankara and Kabir, of Rumi, Lao Tzu and Jesus — I
mention so far Asiatic prophets only [says Coomaraswamy] — can
feel alien to those that have sat at the feet of Kant, Tauler, Behmen
and Ruysbroeck, Whitman, Nietzsche and Blake?"[14] He quotes
Saint Augustine's faith in a "Wisdom Uncreate, the same now as it
ever was, and the same to be for evermore."[15] He points to Chuang
Tzu's cosmopolitanism: "The mind of a sage, being in respose,
becomes the mirror of the entire universe."[16] Referring to the goal
of "self-naughting," of liberation from the bondage of the ego, he
describes Blake as a "prophet of the post-industrial age" and adds,
"It is significant that one could not find in Asiatic scripture a more
typically Asiatic purpose than is revealed in his passionate will to be
delivered from the bondage of division:

> I will go down to self-annihilation and Eternal Death,
> Lest the Last Judgment come and find me unannihilate,
> And I be seized and given into the hands of my own Selfhood."[17]

III   *"Wisdom Is One"*

Though he uses the term "perennial philosophy" in a general
way, Coomaraswamy distinguishes between that philosophy which
is a "wisdom about knowledge" and that which is the wisdom
about the very nature of thought and the nature of the Ultimate
Reality to which thought refers. Perhaps it would be convenient to
use the terms *philosophy* and *wisdom* respectively to refer to the
two types. Philosophies can be plural, Coomaraswamy explains,
but Wisdom can only be one: "Wisdom may be more or less, but
still it is one and the same order of wisdom."[18] There can be Wisdom about different kinds of things (for instance one man may
inquire about the nature of beauty, another about the nature of
truth), but there cannot be different kinds of Wisdom. Sometimes
Coomaraswamy employs a different terminology and calls philosophy "human wisdom" while wisdom is described as First Philosophy. Whatever the terms used, the distinction is stated quite
clearly. Human wisdom deals with "things known or knowable"
and depends on processes of reasoning or dialectic from experi-
mental data. According to Coomaraswamy, "It does not transcend
thought but is rather the best kind of thought, the truest science. It
is indeed an excellent wisdom and, assuming a good will, of great
value to man."[19] It is, however, limited to the field of time and

space, cause and effect, and therefore has to work through "closed systems." "It can affirm or deny nothing with respect to the 'isness' of the infinite in essence,"[20] declares Coomaraswamy.

First Philosophy or Highest Wisdom, however, though it covers the whole ground of human wisdom, goes beyond it and treats confidently of realities which, while they can be viewed as immanent in the space-time tissue, are nevertheless transcendent with respect to that tissue. First Philosophy, states Coomaraswamy, "affirms the actuality of a 'now' independent of flux. It is consistent but not systematic. It is intelligible in itself, though it treats partly of unintelligible things."[21] At its apex, First Philosophy reaches that Ultimate which is its true object. Discerning seers ("visionaries" in the literal sense) have, in all ages and countries, recognized this unity of the ultimate Referent. The Rigvedic "Sat," which is One but "described by poets through different names"; Plutarch's "Logos, known by different epithets"; Apuleius's Isis, "adored in diverse manners" — all these point to the same Supreme which all men seek. Coomaraswamy quotes the comment made by the Mughal emperor, Jahangir, on the Vedantic philosopher Jadrup: "His Vedānta is the same as our *tasawwuf*." He also quotes Dara Shikoh who compiled his Majma-ul-Bahrain (Confluence of Oceans) to show that "there are only verbal differences between the Sufis and the Hindu monotheists." All the paths, then, lead to the summit of the same mountain, concludes Coomaraswamy, "The lower down we are, the more different these paths appear. They vanish at the peak. Each climber will take the one that starts from the point at which he finds himself. He who goes round the mountain looking for another path is not climbing."[22]

At one time, Coomaraswamy reminds us, Christianity also recognized the validity of different paths leading to the same summit. Many Christian thinkers accepted the possibility that the highest truth might have been revealed to exceptional men even before the coming of Jesus Christ. "All that is true, by whomsoever it has been revealed," said Saint Ambrose, "is from the Holy Ghost." And Meister Eckhart spoke of Plato as "that great Priest who found the Way ere ever Christ was born." Even Saint Thomas conceded that the works of Greek and Roman philosophers contain "probable proofs of the truths of Christianity." In course of time, however, Christianity began to arrogate to itself the position of the "only true faith." Plato was replaced by Aristotle as the official philosopher of Christianity, and a line of demarcation was drawn between the "rationalism" of Christianity and the "superstition" of Paganism. Christianity ceased to share with other spiritual traditions the Perennial Philosophy which it had once accepted. Today the position is that, in Coomaraswamy's words, "Hardly two consecutive sentences from Meister Eckhart's sermons would be intelligible to an average modern congregation."[23]

Coomaraswamy's distinction between human wisdom and First Philosophy is in line with the Two Perspectives doctrine of Madhyamika and Advaita Vedanta, the two dominant schools of Buddhist and Hindu thought respectively. It would be useful to restate Coomaraswamy's interpretation of traditional wisdom in terms of these two systems — particularly the latter. This restatement would also lead to an examination of the relation between metaphysics and religion, and of the validity of ethical, social, and aesthetic distinctions in the context of a monistic metaphysic. Before I turn to this question, however, I would like to refer to the views of two outstanding contemporaries of Coomaraswamy who shared his estimate of the perennial philosophy: Aldous Huxley and Rene Guenon.

IV *Coomaraswamy, Huxley, and Guenon*

Huxley and Coomaraswamy have referred to each other in many of their writings. While Coomaraswamy's world view took shape quite early in his career, Huxley came to the perennial philosophy comparatively late in his life. From his earlier novels he emerges as a humanist who views religion and mysticism with an open mind but without much enthusiasm. His humanism is not without a touch of skepticism, sometimes even irony. But his later novels, like *Eyeless in Gaza* and *After Many a Summer Dies the Swan* indicate a change of emphasis. His exposure to oriental philosophies, particularly Buddhism and the dialogues of Shri Ramakrishna, roused his dormant interest in religion — not organized religion, with its hierarchies and its injunctions, but the inward experience which points to a reality higher than that with which we ordinarily deal. In his Preface to the English translation of the teachings of Ramakrishna, Huxley describes the formally illiterate but spiritually enlightened Indian saint as a model of humility and wisdom and as a delightful representative of the perennial philosophy.[24]

Aldous Huxley's *Perennial Philosophy* (1944) is a selection of passages from leaders of religious and philosophical thought in all ages, in the East as well as West. The book is, however, much more than a mere anthology. The selected passages are arranged by subject, and Huxley makes some extremely insightful comments while introducing these various sections. Moreover, in his Introduction to this volume he gives a clear and concise statement of the meaning and implications of the perennial philosophy — a statement which accords quite closely with Coomaraswamy's exposition. He describes *Philosophia Perennis* as "the metaphysic that recognises a Divine Reality substantial to the world of things and lives and minds; the psychology that finds in the soul something similar to, or even identical with, divine Reality; the ethic that places man's final end in the knowledge of the immanent and transcendent Ground of all being."[25] Although the phrase "perennial philosophy" was coined by Leibnitz, the tradition itself is "immemorial and universal." Huxley, like Coomaraswamy, claims that rudiments of the perennial philosophy can be found not only in its developed forms in the higher religions but also in the "traditionary lore of primitive peoples in every region of the world."[26]

In making his selection, Huxley deliberately avoids the writings of the professional philosophers. Explaining this action, he says, "The Perennial Philosophy is primarily concerned with the one divine Reality.... But the nature of this Reality is such that it cannot be directly or immediately apprehended except by those who have chosen to fulfil certain conditions, making themselves loving, pure in heart and poor in spirit." These conditions are rarely fulfilled by academic philosophers. They talk about the subject matter of the perennial philosophy "at second hand." But in almost every age there have been men and women — variously referred to as "sages," "saints," "prophets" or "enlightened ones" — who have given first-hand accounts of that Reality which is the nucleus of the perennial philosophy. Huxley explains, "The self-validating certainty of direct awareness cannot in the very nature of things be achieved except by those equipped with the moral 'astrolabe of God's mysteries.' "[27] It will be seen from these remarks that Aldous Huxley's conception of the perennial philosophy is very similar to that of Coomaraswamy. The only difference is that Coomaraswamy approaches his material as a trained scholar giving careful attention to the etymology of every word from the texts he examines, while Huxley makes no such attempt; and that Coomaraswamy, unlike Huxley, offers a particularly detailed and comprehensive account of the perennial philosophy as expressed in art and aesthetics.

Coomaraswamy was much more directly influenced by Rene Guenon than he was by Aldous Huxley. It is, indeed, a strange coincidence that these two great traditionalists should have independently arrived at almost identical conclusions and then proceeded to strengthen each other's convictions for more than two decades, although they never met personally. After his acquaintance with Rene Guenon's writings, Coomaraswamy's interests gradually shifted to metaphysics in the last fourteen years of his life. Guenon has been justly described as "a catalyst for Coomaraswamy, enabling him to order and relate his vast erudition to timeless principles."[28] In his reviews of Guenon's books, and in some of his own essays, Coomaraswamy has pointed out the deep significance of Guenon's writings. The fact that this significance was missed by the majority of Western scholars is in itself a sad commentary, Coomaraswamy says, on the West's indifference to "first principles."[29] Guenon, in his turn, repeatedly referred to Coomaraswamy's research in support of his interpretations of the perennial philosophy.

In all his books, and particularly in *East and West* and *The Crisis of the Modern World,* Guenon maintains that there is a primordial and universal tradition which is the source of all the major religions of the world, the metaphysical doctrines on which they are founded, and the myths and rituals in which they find expression. This tradition has its own language, the universal language of symbolism, which is not understood by the West in the modern age. In the East these symbols are still embedded in the fabric of human life. Even in the West they are not entirely dead. As Jung has pointed out, they reappear again and again in the dreams and fantasies of Western people. Unfortunately, instead of taking them seriously, they are sought to be explained in terms of the *individual's* "complexes" or unconscious "desires." A few educated Westerners have tried to understand these symbols. But they have done so in the context of all kinds of strange, occult sects. The perennial philosophy cannot be grasped in terms of pseudo-spiritualistic cults. Guenon launches a sharp attack against this trend in some of his books, especially in *Theosophy: The History of a Pseudo-Religion.* Guenon's views on this question are very similar to those of Coomaraswamy, who says that the West can help in "giving the world back its meaning" not by the "assimilation of any surviving oriental patterns but by a recognition of the *principles* on which these patterns are based."[30]

Guenon, like Coomaraswamy, criticizes the attempt of many Western scholars to build an antithesis between reason and intuition and shows that each has its legitimate role in traditional philosophy. Like Coomaraswamy, again, Guenon questions the value of "research for its own sake," unillumined by any goal. Accumulation of data, here and there punctuated by wild guesses, is often sanctimoniously described as "research." This is one of the symptoms of the "mental restlessness" that the West is experiencing as a result of the breakdown of traditional society which had "ordered means" and clearly perceived ends. "Forgetting the 'Seek and ye shall find' of the Gospels, the modern Westerner seems to seek merely for the sake of seeking," says Coomaraswamy; "he is almost afraid of finding anything real and final, for he gives the name of 'death' to whatever constitutes a definite finality and the name of 'life' to what is really no more than aimless agitation."[31]

The two thinkers thus had much in common. Coomaraswamy said that he agreed with Guenon entirely on metaphysical principles and differed only on minor points. The difference between them is one of style rather than of substance. Guenon's writings have a kind of icy glitter appropriate to the higher Himalayas, while Coomaraswamy's have the warm glow of the Gangetic valley.[32] Their respective contributions can be summed up in this comment made by an outstanding scholar who admired both of them: "Guenon is like the vertical axis of a cross fixed with mathematical precision on immutable realities and their immediate applications in cosmological sciences. Ananda Coomaraswamy is the horizontal complement, expanding these truths over the vast field of arts, cultures, mythologies and symbolism — metaphysical truths on the one hand, and universal beauty on the other."[33]

V *Metaphysics and Religion*

It now becomes necessary to relate in somewhat greater detail Coomaraswamy's views on fundamental questions — views based upon the perennial philosophy, views which (as already emphasized) are not his own, "except in the sense that I have made them my own." Since metaphysics is the focal point of the traditional philosophy, one must begin with Coomaraswamy's exposition of metaphysical doctrine. The first point to be taken up in this connection is the relationship between metaphysics and religion, both of which lean on revelation.

"Our problem," says Coomaraswamy, "is to *distinguish without dividing* religion from metaphysics.... It is a distinction without a difference, like that of attribute from essence."[34] Failure to grasp this distinction is responsible for serious misunderstandings of the perennial philosophy, especially as expressed in the Indian tradition. Religion proceeds "from the being in act" (kāryāvasthā) of the First Principle without reference to its "being in potentiality" (kāranāvasthā). Metaphysics treats of the Supreme Identity as "unity of potentiality and act." Religion assumes an aspect of duality, for example in postulating primary matter or non-being as far removed from the actuality of God. Metaphysics supersedes such duality. It follows that religions can be (and are) many, each being an "arrangement of God," and stylistically differentiated. "He takes the forms imagined by His worshippers," states Coomaraswamy. Hence religious beliefs can unite but also divide. The major religions of the world have given rise to tolerance as well as intolerance; metaphysics, however, can only unite.

The most urgent task of philosophy, therefore, is to demonstrate the common metaphysical basis of all religions and diverse cultures. Coomaraswamy attaches the greatest importance to this function of philosophy. He urges philosophers to "control and revise the principles of comparative religion." Only under the guidance of philosophy can a man learn to say "My religion is the best for me" rather than "My religion is the best." The true purpose of religious debate or controversy is not to convert the opponent but rather to persuade him that his religion is essentially the same as ours: in other words, to convince him that he is not our opponent at all.[35] But this is a view which religious dogmatists, particularly in the camp of Christianity, look upon with horror. In dogmatic religion there is an element of fear that the discovery of the truth might upset one's own faith. One of the functions of philosophy is to dissipate such fears, declares Coomaraswamy: "Only metaphysics, which is the basis and norm of all religious formulations, can provide the ground for agreement. Once a common ground is recognised, it is simple to 'agree to disagree' regarding details. Only metaphysics can convince the adherents of all religions that divergent formulations (dharmaparyāya) are no more than paraphrases of one and the same principle."[36]

For both metaphysics and religion man's last end is the realization by the individual of all the possibilities inherent in his own being. Men of discernment in all ages have understood this. The neo-Platonists, Augustine, Erigena and Eckhart, Rumi and Ibn-al-Arabi and Shankara — they all knew that "religious and intellectual experience is too closely interwoven ever to be wholly divided," and that "the Way of Gnosis and the Way of Participation are one." A return to the traditional, integrated world view enables us to realize, however, that this oneness does not preclude distinctions: those, for instance, betwen Christianity and Gnosticism, Sunni and Shi'a doctrines, Ramanuja and Shankara. Such differences of viewpoint and emphasis arise from the fact that in life, as experienced, there are real distinctions of Will and Intellect, participation and apprehension, "knowledge-of" and "knowledge-as" (aparā vidyā and parā vidyā). In a further comment on the distinction between metaphysics and religion, Coomaraswamy says, "As regards the Way, the distinction is one of consecration from initiation, of passive from active integration. As regards the End, the distinction is one of assimilation from identification."[37] The demand of religion is "Perfect yourself"; the demand of metaphysics is "Realise your own perfection." To religion, sin is moral; to metaphysics it is intellectual (assertion of independent self-subsistence). Both, regarded as proximately distinct but ultimately identical, have the same central aim. "Both, as Ways or as Praxes, can accomplish rectification, regeneration and reintegration of the aberrant, fragmented individual consciousness,"[38] says Coomaraswamy.

It should be noted here (though this is a point to which we shall soon return) that Coomaraswamy's distinction between metaphysics and religion is implied in the position of Advaita Vedanta regarding the distinction between two valid perspectives: the transcendental (pāramārthika) and the empirical (vyāvahārika). Shankara, the most outstanding representative of this point of view, advocates a philosophy of absolute monism and at the same time vigorously denies the charge that such a philosophy "makes the world disappear." He gives full recognition to the religious, ethical, and social distinctions on which the practical life of man is based. While maintaining that ultimately even God (Ishvara) must be regarded as an appearance, and that Reality in the strict sense can be ascribed only to the Absolute (Brahman), he calls for a conscientious performance of religious ritual and even composed devotional hymns for the worship of a personal God, who must indeed be accepted as the Creator, Preserver, and Destroyer of the world. And the phenomenal world itself, though an appearance, is an

appearance *of the Real* and must be taken seriously while we are
still "on this shore."

VI   *Reality*

Coomaraswamy awards primacy to metaphysics and looks upon
the concept of Reality as basic to the traditional philosophy which
he expounds. The following passage, taken from one of his last and
most mature writings, may serve as a convenient statement of this
concept: "God is an essence without duality (advaita) or, as some
maintain, without duality but not without relations (vishishtād-
vaita). He is only to be apprehended as Essence (asti), but this
essence subsists in a twofold nature (dvaitībhāva), as being and as
becoming. Thus what is called the Entirety (kritsnam, pūrnam,
bhūman) is both explicit and inexplicit (niruktānirukta), sonant
and silent (shabdāshabda), characterized and uncharacterized
(saguna, nirguna), temporal and eternal (kālākala), partite and
impartite, in a likeness and not in any likeness (mūrtamūrta),
shown and unshown (vyaktāvyakta), mortal and immortal
(martyāmartya), and so forth."[39]
Here Coomaraswamy describes Reality — or rather indicates its
nature, since it is indescribable — in the language of the Upanishads. The ascription of apparently contradictory attributes is one
of the devices which the sages of the Upanishads employ to suggest
two ideas: first, that the finite human intellect is caught up in
antinomies when it tries to fathom the Absolute; and second, that
the Infinite contains as well as transcends all the categories through
which it can possibly be communicated. Hence the *Katha Upanishad* calls the Real "smaller than the smallest, greater than the
greatest"; and again, "Though seated, He travels far; though at
rest, He moves all things.... Formless is He, though inhabiting
form. In the midst of the fleeting He abides for ever." Not only in
the Upanishads but even in the theistic devotional hymns Ultimate
Reality is referred to as indescribable. To call it "indescribable" is
itself a description, but this dilemma simply cannot be overcome,
unless we are satisfied with "description through pure silence."
Coomaraswamy quotes the Shaiva hymnist, Manikka Vachagar:
"He is passing the description of words, not comprehensible to the
mind, not visible to the eye or other senses." And yet the same poet
proceeds to offer vivid pen pictures of that which can be "neither
sung nor sketched" for the benefit of the worshipper.[40]

The way of negation and the way of contradiction are, thus, not the only alternatives to utter silence. There is also the urge to communicate the Real through symbols. The names and forms ascribed to the Supreme are to be taken as the results of this urge towards symbolic expression. The symbol may, however, be one in which all names and forms are condensed. The sacred syllable "Om" is such a condensation. Explaining the importance of "Om" in the Vedic tradition, Coomaraswamy says, "Of all the names and forms of God, the monogrammatic syllable Om, the totality of all sounds ... is the best. The validity of such an audible symbol is exactly the same as that of an icon, both alike serving as supports of contemplation (*dhīyālamba*). Such a support is needed because that which is imperceptible to eye or ear cannot be apprehended objectively as it is in itself, but only in a likeness."[41] A symbol cannot be selected casually or arbitrarily, says Coomaraswamy. "It must be naturally adequate, and cannot be chosen at random; one infers (*āveshyati, āvāhayati*) the unseen in the seen, the unheard in the heard." And yet, however perfect the symbol, it is after all just that, a likeness. "These forms are only means by which to approach the formless, and must be discarded before we become it,"[42] says Coomaraswamy. All methods of communicating the Incommunicable — negative, paradoxical, or symbolic, visual, auditory, or imaginative — have a purely functional validity at the phenomenal level, while the knower of the Real has not yet *become* the Real, and therefore has not even become the knower in the true sense.

In his exposition of Buddhism Coomaraswamy shows that this notion of Reality as One, transcendental and indescribable is fully accepted in Mahayana philosophy, particularly in Nāgārjuna's Shūnyavāda and "Mind-only" school of Yogāchāra. The approach to Reality through negations and paradoxes is used with great skill in Nāgārjuna's dialectics. He examines the four categories of the intellect (existence, nonexistence, both-existence-and-nonexistence, neither-existence-nor-nonexistence) which operate in the world of phenomena and can give us only relative concepts. In its essential nature, the Real is empty of all determinations. The *Shūnya* (Void or Emptiness) indicates the fact that Reality cannot be grasped through the conceptual or linguistic equipment of the finite mind. It does *not* imply nihilism. When the Ultimate Reality is emptied of all the qualities which are ascribed to it by the intellect, it shines by its own pure light. Emptiness is thus the same as Suchness or Thatness (*Tathatā*) which is existence-in-itself. From the relative point of view, Reality is *Shūnya;* but actually even this epithet cannot be applied to it. Coomaraswamy quotes Nāgārjuna's verse justifying the use of the word *Shūnya:* "It cannot be called Void, or not Void, or both, or neither. But simply in order to indicate it, it is called The Void." In the Yogāchāra concept of *Alaya Vijnāna* (Receptacle Consciousness), the same conclusion is reached by a different road. The emphasis, again, is on the relative and transient nature of all phenomenal things. Reality, if it can be indicated at all, must be regarded as Absolute Consciousness. The fact is that all the concepts in Buddhism converge ultimately at one point where the divergent emphases which they carry dissolve into a single idea of the Absolute. *Prajnā* (Wisdom), *Tathatā* (Suchness), Nirvāna, *Karunā* (Compassion), *Shūnya, Alayavijnāna,* even the Buddha — not the historical person but the Buddha-essence — point to the same reality. All multiplicity belongs to the world of appearance, of manifestation. The Real remains One.

Although Coomaraswamy does not consistently use the words *Absolute* and *God* to indicate the unmanifest and the manifest aspects of the One, respectively, he accepts this distinction as one of the common features of the perennial philosophy. The position is, in his words, "stated with rigorous exactitude" in the Vedānta of Samkara. *Ishvara,* or personal God, the creator, sustainer and destroyer of the phenomenal universe (or rather universes) is only the manifested aspect of Brahman. Strictly speaking, it is only to Ishvara that the qualities of *Sat, Chit* and *Ananda* (Existence, Consciousness, Bliss) should be attributed. These are the highest qualities which the human imagination can think of in conjuring up a vision of perfection. They are superimposed (*adhyāropa*) by the finite upon the Infinite. God or Ishvara is Identity seen as Identity-in-difference. Since the finite mind cannot grasp Brahman as Pure Being, such a superimposition is inescapable from the practical viewpoint (Vyāvahārika drishti). Ishvara is the source of moral and aesthetic value, the object or focal point of religious adoration. A further differentiation, prompted by the religious yearnings of human individuals, leads to the recognition of many forms of Ishvara himself. Krishna, Rāma and other deities are aspects of the manifested Ishvara, as Ishvara himself is an aspect of the unmanifest Brahman. "The Hindu religion," Coomaraswamy points out, "adapts itself with infinite grace to every human need."[43] Reality is described in terms of the ideal attainable by the individual at the spiritual level where he happens to be at a given moment. When the level changes, the ideal becomes higher, declares Coomaraswamy. "The Hindu Ishvara is not a jealous God because all gods are aspects of Him, imagined by his worshippers. In the words of Krishna: 'When any devotee seeks to worship any aspect with faith, it is none other than Myself that bestows the steadfast faith, and when by worshipping any aspect he wins what he desires, it is none other than Myself that grants his prayers. Howsoever men approach me, so do I welcome them, for the path men take from every side is mine.' "[44] Coomaraswamy gives special praise to Hinduism for refusing to reject any mode of offering homage to the Divine: "The collective genius that made Hinduism a continuity ranging from the contemplation of the Absolute to the physical service of an image made of clay did not shrink from an ultimate acceptance of every aspect of God conceived by man, and of every ritual devised by his devotion."[45]

In Western religions prior to the Renaissance Coomaraswamy sees ample corroboration of this view of Reality as the foundation of the perennial philosophy. After quoting the Upanishadic statement that when all attributes are negated one reaches the Unity of the Person, he says, "This text agrees with the *via negativa* of neo-Platonic and Christian theologians." He refers to Nicholas of Cusa who declared that "the Wall of Paradise is built of contradictions," and to Dante's statement that "what lies beyond is not in space, nor has it poles" and that "every 'when' and every 'where' is combined in it." Among others in the Western tradition to whom Coomaraswamy has referred in various contexts as expressing views of the Absolute that are fundamentally the same as those found in the Upanishads, Buddhism and, Vedanta, mention need be made only of Philo, Dionysius the Areopagite, Ruysbroeck, and Meister Eckhart. Philo, describing the Absolute as beyond attributes, says, "He who thinks that God has any qualities and is not One injures not God but himself." Dionysius the Areopagite speaks of the "superluminous darkness" in which the mystery of Divine Truth is hidden. "This darkness, though of deepest obscurity, is yet radiantly clear; and, though beyond touch and sight, it fills our unseeing minds with splendors of transcendent beauty.... For this is truly to see and to know and, through the abandonment of all things, to praise Him who is above and beyond all things." Almost in the exact language of Vedanta, Dionysius goes on to say that if we ascribe attributes to Him we come down from the Universal to the particulars, whereas by "taking away all things from Him" we proceed from the particulars to the Universals, "that we may know openly the Unknowable."

Corresponding to Samkara's distinction between Brahman and Ishvara, we have Ruysbroeck's distinction between the Godhead and God. "There is a differentiation, according to our Reason," he says, "between God and the Godhead, between action and rest. The fruitful nature of the Persons ever worketh in a living distinction. But the simple being of God, according to the nature thereof, is an eternal Rest of God and of all created things." In the state of identity with Reality, Ruysbroeck says, "we can speak no more of the Father, Son and Holy Spirit, nor of any creature, but only one Being, which is the very substance of the Divine Person. There were we all one before our creation, for this is our super-essence. There the Godhead is in simple essence without activity." But the closest parallel between the Indian and the Western concept of Reality can be seen in the utterances of Meister Eckhart, to whom Coomaraswamy has devoted special attention. "I beseech you by the eternal and imperishable truth," Eckhart implores, "and by my soul, to consider, to grasp the unheard-of. God and Godhead are as distinct as heaven and earth. Heaven stands a thousand miles above earth, and even so the Godhead is above God. God becomes and disbecomes. Whoever understands this teaching, I wish him well. But even if nobody had been here, I must still have preached it to the poor-box." The Christian missionaries in nineteenth-century India, who were shocked to find in the highest school of Hindu philosophy the doctrine that God is an appearance which must be left behind, were apparently not familiar with the teachings of Meister Eckhart.

VII   *The Self and Selves*

This pure Being, the ground which cannot be fathomed even through the notion of God, is visualized as Supreme Consciousness, the source of all knowledge which can therefore never become the object of knowledge. This is the Self. What is referred to as Brahman, viewed objectively, is called Atman when the gaze is turned inward. It is the primordial and present witness, the subtle essence that pervades all things.[46] Some of the most stirring metaphors in the Upanishads are those in which the highest Self is eulogized. As rivers, flowing from different sides, find their rest in the ocean, leaving their forms and names behind, so do all beings, released from names and forms, go to the Self, which is "beyond the beyond." "O Yājnavalkya," the Emperor asks the sage, "when the sun has set, and the moon does not shine, and the fires have gone out, and there is not even a sound, then by what light can the truth be known?" And the teacher answers: "It is the Atman, the Self, which then becomes the light." Then there is the famous metaphor of the chariot: "The body is the chariot. The mind is the driver. The intellect is the bridle. The senses are the horses. The objects of sense are the fields and roads. And the Atman, the Self, is the Master who enjoys the drive without moving."

The doctrine about the Self is, in Coomaraswamy's words, the "pivot around which the traditional wisdom of India revolves." In the *Bhagavadgītā,* the most popular of Hindu scriptures, the Upanishadic teaching is made the basis of the entire philosophy of life. "The Self does not slay, neither is it slain," Krishna reminds Arjuna, who is overcome by dejection at the thought of shedding the blood of kinsmen. "Weapons cannot cut the Self, fire cannot burn it, water cannot wet it, the wind cannot dry it," adds Krishna. The Self is changeless, all-pervasive, and "altogether ancient." This imperishable reality is the very tissue of the universe. Even the Buddha, far from rejecting the Self, as some interpreters of the *anattā* doctrine assert, actually refers to the Self on several occasions, in spite of his "noble silence" on metaphysical questions. In the Buddha's sermons, Coomaraswamy points out, the Self is established by the same process of elimination that was adopted in the Upanishads: "Our own constitution and that of the world is repeatedly analysed. As each one of the five physical and mental factors of the transient personality with which the 'untaught many-folk' identify themselves is listed, the pronouncement follows, '*That* is not my self' (*na me so atma*)."[47] We read in the *Dhammapada,* "Let a Bhikkhu reprove himself by the Self, and examine himself by the Self, so that he may live happily." And again: "Self is the Lord of self and the goal of self. What other Lord can there be?" It is of the Self, and not of himself, that the Buddha is speaking when he declares, "I have taken refuge in my Self."

We now come to the most important plank of the *Philosophia Perennis.* This Supreme Spirit, the Self or Atman, is *identified with the One,* the Real, which is variously referred to as Brahman, Godhead, "That," or Absolute. The Upanishadic statement *tat tvam asi* (That thou art) is the clearest and most direct assertion of this iden-

tity. But in the Islamic and the Christian tradition also such an identity has been repeatedly asserted. What is equally important, while
the Self (*Atman*) is identified with the Real (*Brahman*), it is simultaneously dissociated from the individual soul or ego (*Jīva*).
Permanence is asserted of the Self and is denied of the selves. Man
is described as bound, ignorant, helpless only to the extent that he
sees Self in what is not-Self. His actions are *self*-ish (to quote a
Buddhist text) so long as he identifies himself with soul-and-body
(*savinnāna-kaya*). "Material shape is impermanent. What is impermanent, that is suffering. What is suffering, that is not the Self.
What is not Self, that is not mine, that am I not." These words
from the Sanyutta Nikāya[48] show that what the Buddhist rejects is
the transient "bundle" of accidents which we miscall ourselves. In
the Upanishads, a distinction is clearly made between the *Atman* —
the one, universal supreme Self — and the *Bhūtātman,* the individual ego, or "feeling of personal identity" or the "sense of being
oneself."

The question "What am I?" therefore involves the prior question "What is that which seems to be 'me' but really is not?" just as
the question "What is Brahman?" involves the inquiry into what
Brahman is not. The aim of Yoga is precisely this: to neutralize and
then eliminate the confusion resulting from mental modifications
of the Self. The mind, which is a product of phenomenal nature, is
mistaken for the Spirit, which is beyond nature. When this error is
rectified we recognize that our inner essence is identical with the
Self. Coomaraswamy notes two further implications of this distinction. The first is that the Self, which is perfection, cannot be
described as human. "The metaphysical concept of Perfection is a
state of being which is *not inhuman* (because it is accessible to whoever will press inward to the central point of consciousness), but
assuredly non-human,"[49] states Coomaraswamy. That is why in
one of the Upanishads Agni is described as *amānava purusha*
("non-human person") leading the Comprehending One to the far-
ther side. The second implication is that the attainment of the Self
is "death and darkness no less than life and light."[50] The "way of
the gods" (*Devayāna*) "must lead sooner or later to the final death
of the soul." It is therefore incorrect to speak of the "immortality
of the soul" as is done in popular usage; "the soul can be immor-
talized only by returning to its source, that is by dying to itself and
living to its Self." This is the *Fana-al-fana* (total dissolution) of the
Sufis. The liberated in life, the *jīvanmukta* of Hinduism, is dead to

his lower self before he recognizes his identity with the higher. That is why it is said of him that he "dies no more" (*na punarmriyate*). "Having died already, as the Sufi puts it, he is now as a 'dead man walking,' "[51] says Coomaraswamy.

In all traditional philosophies it has therefore been universally recognized that there are two elements in man: his psycho-physical individuality, which functions in the spatial and temporal dimensions; and a fundamental, imperishable element which is the same in every one and is indeed identical with the Ground. Salvation or emancipation — or freedom, or liberation — it does not really matter what term we use — is the recognition of the divine spiritual essence as being different from the mutable (and corruptible) body-and-soul. The metaphysical destiny of every human being is thus trans-human.

Once again Coomaraswamy emphasizes that this doctrine is not exclusively Eastern. Saint Paul made a distinction between the soul and the spirit. The idea that "the soul must put itself to death" is shared by Christian, Hindu, and Muslim mystics. Meister Eckhart speaks of an "outward man" and an "inner man." "To the outward man belong those things that depend on the soul, but are connected with the flesh and are blended with it.... But within us all there is the other person, whom the Scripture calls the new man, the heavenly man," says Eckhart. He refers to the spirit within us as "the seed of God." "Given an intelligent and hard-working farmer, it will thrive and grow up to God, whose seed it is," he adds; "and accordingly its fruits will be God-nature. Pear seeds grow into pear trees, nut seeds into nut trees, God-seed into God." In an even more remarkable passage Eckhart writes, "There is a spirit in the soul, untouched by time and flesh, flowing from the Spirit, remaining in the Spirit. In this principle is God, ever verdant, ever flowering in all the joy and glory of His actual Self." Eckhart goes on to say that at one time he used to call this principle within each man by various names: "Tabernacle of the Soul," "Spiritual Light," a "Spark." "But now I say that it is more exalted than all this.... So now I name it in a nobler fashion.... It is free of all names and void of all forms. It is one and simple, as God is one and simple, and no one can in any wise behold it," Eckhart concludes.

The German mystic of the thirteenth century was thus saying almost the same thing that the sages of the Upanishads had said two thousand years earlier: that there is an essence within us

(Atman) which, like Godhead (Brahman), is one, invisible, devoid of name and form, indescribable, the source of all joy, the supreme consciousness; and that this essence is *not* our body, mind, or ego. Another writer frequently quoted by Coomaraswamy is William Law. "God is present to thee," says Law,

in the deepest and most central part of thy soul. The natural senses cannot possess God or unite thee to Him; nay, even thy inward faculties of understanding, will and memory can only reach after God, but cannot be the place of his habitation in thee. But there is a root or depth of thee from whence all these faculties come forth, as lines from a center, or as branches from the body of the tree. This depth is called the center, the fund or bottom of the soul. This depth is the unity, the eternity — I had almost said the Infinity — of thy soul; for it is so infinite that nothing can satisfy it or give it rest but the infinity of God.

Law *almost* identifies the human spirit with God. He just stops short of doing so and contents himself by saying that it is very close to God's infinity. While Eckhart seems to have reached the position of absolute monism, like Samkara in his interpretation of "tat tvam asi" (That thou art), William Law seems, like Rāmānuja, to speak of unity but hesitates to proclaim absolute identity. In the East as well as in the West, Coomaraswamy points out, such differences fall within the framework of the perennial philosophy. Some wish to preserve relations, but not duality; others soar even higher and speak of a totally nonrelational unity. In either case the oneness of the Whole is assumed, and so is the distinction between the imperishable divine essence and the perishable personality-structure within each finite center.

VIII *Immortality and Transmigration*

Immortality, in one form or another, is assumed to be an undeniable fact in all traditional philosophies and the religions based upon them. In India there is also the distinctive notion of rebirth or transmigration. It is by no means an exclusively Indian notion, having been accepted by the Pythagoreans and many other religious groups in the ancient and medieval West. But it has a special significance in the Indian tradition, particularly because of the close connection between the Law of Karma and the assumption of life after death. Both these ideas go back to pre-Aryan times and we know of no age in Indian history when they were not prevalent.

Coomaraswamy's emphasis, on this question, is on distinguishing the popular from the orthodox concepts of immortality and rebirth.

The Higher Wisdom or the First Philosophy is, in its very nature, concerned primarily with immaterial things; and it is only in regard to these that the question of immortality arises. Material things are obviously not immortal as such. They are subject to flux and are constantly being modified. "There may be some immortal principle in them — but if so, it must be eternally so. An immortal principle cannot *become* mortal. If it does, it never was immortal," says Coomaraswamy.[52] To describe any one as having "become immortal" can therefore be permissible only in popular usage. This usage reflects the tenacious notion that somehow our individual consciousness (including memory, character, etc.) survives after death, "just as it survives after nightly intervals from day to day."[53] When one is asked to justify the idea of immortality, two positions are ordinarily taken: first, while frankly admitting that the only possible immortality is through memories of other mortal beings, one might search for proofs of the existence of individuals or groups who have been forgotten for millenia, but who have been "reincarnated." The reincarnation visualized here is based on the idea that there must be some imperishable quality about these men which enabled their name and fame to withstand the obliterating process of time. This type of immortality, merely through the memories of those who come after us, does not, however, seem to satisfy most of us: this is not the "everlasting life" we fondly hope for. The second type of attempt to "prove" immortality is linked with the search for evidence of communication from the other world, establishing continuity of memory and persistence of character after the death of the body. Such attempts are said to be successful when it is shown that there are manifestations of one sort or another, kinds of matter subtler than and different from those we perceive by our senses; or that our consciousness continues — after its connection with the body is broken — to function on other planes of being.[54]

Both these concepts are about our consciousness, that is about finite individual selves. They are intended to be rationalistic interpretations of immortality, and Coomaraswamy emphasizes that they are totally rejected by both metaphysics and religion: "The *possibility* of indefinite persistence of individual consciousness on various platforms of being, and in various temporal modes, is not denied in religion or metaphysics. But persistence in such modes is *not the same as Immortality.*"[55] Coomaraswamy refers to the idea of "aeviternity" in this context. "Metaphysics and religion do allow," he says, "that there may be states of being not wholly in time, nor yet in eternity (in the sense of the 'timeless now'), but aeviternal." The Vedic term *amritatva* suggests aeviternity rather than immortality: "a mean between time and eternity." Angels or *devas* are looked upon as "conscious intellectual substances, eternal in their immutable nature and understanding, but of time as regards their accidental awareness of before and after, and the changeability of their affections."[56] Coomaraswamy quotes passages from Philo, Rumi, and various Upanishads to show the universally prevalent belief that some men "could be regarded as partaking in aeviternal being" or "being taken into angelic orders." But this is not immortality in the deeper sense.

What, then, must we understand by immortality? The question can be answered, Coomaraswamy insists, only by clarifying the notion of time: "The metaphysical doctrine simply contrasts time as a continuum with the eternity that is not in time and so cannot properly be called *everlasting,* but coincides with the real present or 'now' of which temporal experience is impossible." The confusion arises because, "for a consciousness functioning in time and space 'now' succeeds 'now' without interruption, and there seems to be an endless series of 'nows,' collectively adding up to 'time.' " The confusion can be eliminated "by realizing that none of these 'nows' has any duration and that, as measures, all alike are zeros, of which a sum is unthinkable." Time or temporal sequence is thus relative; its impact is upon us, placed as we are in the empirical world, and we understand it in terms of our own finite perspective. "It is we who move," says Coomaraswamy, "while the Now is unmoved and only seems to move, as the sun only seems to rise and set because the earth revolves."[57]

In the *Bhagavadgītā,* when Arjuna requests Krishna to appear in his divine form, the Lord reveals himself as one in whom the past, the present, and the future are held together simultaneously and in whom the vast cosmic spaces are annihilated. All exponents of the perennial philosophy assert, in various ways, the central truth that distinctions of time and space apply only to the finite and not to the infinite. "Since God hath always an eternal and present state," says Boethius, "His knowledge, surpassing time's notions, remaineth in the simplicity of His presence and, comprehending the infinity of what is past and to come considereth all things as though they were in the act of being accomplished." What is ordinarily called God's foreknowledge "is in reality a timeless now-knowledge." The finite notion of time must therefore be transcended if one is to recognize the infinite in its essence. In a beautiful stanza, Jalal-al-Din Rumi says, "Burn up the past, burn up the future! They veil God from our sight. How long will you be partitioned into these segments, like a reed? So long as a reed is partitioned, it will not respond to lip or breath." In the same vein Eckhart says that "time is what keeps the light from reaching us. There is no greater obstacle to God than time. And not only time but temporalities, not only temporal things but temporal affections; not only only temporal affections but the very taint and smell of time."

The idea of immortality, then, is not offered to man as a comforting assurance that he will somehow circumvent the law of impermanence. On the contrary, it tells him that only by dying completely to his finite self can he identify himself with the eternal ground of all existence: "What metaphysics understands by Immortality and Eternity implies and demands of every man a total, uncompromising denial of himself and a final mortification, to be dead and buried in the Godhead."[58] Coomaraswamy quotes this passage from the *Brihadāranyaka Upanishad:* "Whoever realises this, avoids contingent death (*punarmrityu*). Death gets him not, for Death becomes his essence." That is to say, the knowledge of his own essence is bound up with the destruction of his finitude. And with this knowledge comes the realization that mortality belongs to the world of appearance. The prayer "From the unreal lead me to the real" is the same as the prayer "From death lead me to immortality" and "From darkness lead me to light." Only eternity is real; mortality, or impermanence, is unreal.[59] "Here in this ego-conscious world we are subject to mortality. But this mortality is an illusion, and all its truths are relative. Over against this world of change and separation there is a timeless and spaceless peace which is the source and goal of all our being — "that noble Pearl," in the words of Behmen, 'which to the World appears Nothing, but to the Children of Wisdom is All Things.' "[60]

The popular notion of transmigration is based on the idea that immortality means the persistence of the "soul" in its finite career, clothed in some other body. This, Coomaraswamy insists, is *not* the orthodox Hindu doctrine according to which "there is no transmigrant other than the Lord, who is at once transcendent and inherent in relation to all beings without ever transforming Himself into any of them." The popular belief is seized upon by critics of the orthodox tradition; and all sorts of crude ideas, associated with transmigration, are publicized as proofs of the backwardness and irrationalism of Hinduism. These critics fail to grasp the fact that behind these ideas there is the clear assertion of the Supreme Self as the *only* reality to which immortality can be ascribed. Coomaraswamy writes, "All traditional texts ... which *seem* to assert a reincarnation of individual essences are expressions, in terms of a popular pragmatic animism, — 'animistic' in the sense that they assume the reality of the postulated Ego — and should be assumed metaphysically as having reference only to the universality of the immanent Spirit, Daimon, or Eternal Man-in-this-man who realizes his own extempore omnipresence when he 'reassumes his ancient bliss.' "[61]

Enlightenment, therefore, is invariably accompanied by an attitude of quiet unconcern with reincarnation in the sense of survival after death. "Seeing Him alone," says the *Shvetāshvatara Upanishad,* "one transcends death. There is no other way." And the *Yogavasishtha* says that survival in bodily form makes no difference whatsoever: "Troubled or still, water is always water. What difference can embodiment or disembodiment make to the liberated? Whether calm or in tempest, the sameness of the ocean suffers no change." A clear distinction must therefore be made between *survival,* which implies persistence in time in one form or another, and *immortality,* which is participation in the Absolute's eternal "now." Meister Eckhart says, "I already possess all that is granted to me in eternity; for God, in the fulness of his Godhead dwells eternally in his image — the soul." Such being the case, it is not for the survival of the soul in some separate form but rather for its *non-survival* that the wise man should aspire. And this brings us back to the idea that dying to the phenomenal state is the same as living in the transcendental.

Many poets and mystics, in all ages and countries, have expressed this thought, but few have done so more beautifully than Rumi:

I died a clod of matter and became a plant. I died a plant and rose to be an animal. Dying as an animal, I then became a man. Why, then, should I be afraid? Did I ever suffer diminution by dying? Once again shall I die, as a man, to become an angel and soar with other blessed angels. But I must pass on. Even my angelic state must I relinquish. Since God alone is imperishable, I must surely sacrifice my angel-soul. Then shall I soar higher and become that which no mind has ever conceived, or ever shall conceive. O, let me exist no more! Non-existence proclaims loudly: 'To Him shall we return.'

IX *Ethics*

Eternity, or the state of liberation from finitude and change, is the ultimate goal of all human endeavor. Right conduct, based on discrimination between right and wrong, is a part of that total endeavor. In all traditional world views, ethics is inseparably bound up with metaphysics on the one hand and social thought on the other. The former aspect of morality makes it the science of Self-realization (*Adhyātma-vidyā*); the latter, representing "right living," can only be considered in terms of one's own place in the world, determined by one's temperament, ability, aptitude, and vocation. I will, therefore, deal with the practical implications of traditional ethics in the chapter on social thought. *Dharma,* which is as much ethics as religion, cannot be considered apart from what is proper and good for the community. In Plato's concept of justice, and in the Hindu stress on *Svadharma* (one's own duty), this attitude of the perennial philosophy to ethical questions becomes quite apparent. A few general observations, however, appear to be appropriate at this point.

The following passage from Aldous Huxley gives an accurate idea of the traditional attitude to the good: "For the perennial philosophy, good is the separate self's conformity to, and finally annihilation in, the divine Ground which gives it being; evil is the intensification of separateness, the refusal to know that the Ground exists. This doctrine is, of course, perfectly compatible with the formulation of ethical principles as a series of negative and positive divine commandments, or even in terms of social utility."[62] Goodness or badness of one's actions (and thought, too, is a kind of activity), depends upon which part of oneself is in command. "People should think less about what they ought to *do,*" says Meister Eckhart, "and more about what they ought to *be.* If only their being were good, their works would shine forth brightly.... Salvation rests on what you *are.*" We are thus back at the distinction between the Self and the self within us. "The good man," says William Law, "is one who concurs with the living, inspiring spirit of God within him; and the bad man is one who resists it.... Your own self is the Cain that murders your own Abel."

Coomaraswamy explains this idea with reference to the traditional Hindu distinction between the Way of Desire and the Way of Renunciation. "The life or lives of men," says Coomaraswamy, "may be regarded as constituting a curve — an arc of time-experience subtended by the duration of the individual Will to Life. The outward movement on this curve — Evolution, the Path of Pursuit (*Pravritti Mārga*), is characterized by self-assertion. The inward movement — Involution, the Path of Return (*Nivritti Mārga*), is characterized by increasing Self-realization. The religion of men on the outward path is the Religion of Time; the religion of those who return is the Religion of Eternity."[63] It should be clarified that Coomaraswamy uses the word *evolution* in the sense of the expression of one's "tendencies" in the external world, and that the word *religion* as used here refers to Dharma, which includes Duty or "Truth in living" in addition to what is commonly meant by "religion."

And just because the religion of eternity culminates in the knowledge of identity between the Self within us and the divine Ground, between the Atman and the Brahman, ethics must inevitably be transcended in the state of liberation. One of the criticisms leveled against Hinduism by nineteenth-century Western scholars was its alleged indifference to Ethics. It was alleged that the concept of *Moksha* is destructive of the ultimacy of ethical value. It is, however, by no means peculiar to Hinduism to think of salvation as a trans-ethical state. Indeed, this is an inescapable corollary of the perennial philosophy. The truths of ethics, like those of theology itself, are relative. Ethical conduct, like any other rite, can only be a means to the highest end. Explaining this point of view, which is involved as much in the Christian as the Hindu myth, Coomaraswamy says, "As it was by the knowledge of good and evil that man fell from his high estate, so it must be from the knowledge of good and evil, from the moral law, that he must be delivered at last. However far one may have gone, there remains a last step to be taken, involving a dissolution of all former values. A church or society that does not provide a way of escape from its own regiment, and will not let its people go, is defeating its own purpose."[64]

Even Buddhism, which was once regarded as an "ethical code rather than a religious doctrine" adopts the same point of view. "The Buddha himself," Coomaraswamy points out, "does not attach an absolute value to moral conduct. We must not suppose that because the means are partly ethical Nirvana is therefore an ethical state. So far from this, un-self-ishness, from the Indian point of view, is an amoral state, in which no question of 'altruism' can present itself, liberation being as much from the notion of 'others' as it is from the notion of 'self.' 'I call him a Brāhman indeed,' says the Buddha, who has passed beyond attachment both to good and evil, 'one who is clean, to whom no dust attaches, who is a-pathetic.' "[65] Coomaraswamy interprets the famous Buddhist parable of the raft as a confirmation of the trans-ethical nature of Nirvana. By the raft of virtue one crosses the river of life. But the Buddha pointedly asks, "What does a man do with the boat when he has reached the other side of the river? Does he carry it about on his back, or does he leave it on the shore?" Perfection is more than innocence, declares Coomaraswamy. "There must be knowledge of what are folly and wisdom, good and evil, and of how to be rid of *both* these values, wrong and 'right without being righteous' (shīlavat no cha shīlamayah). For the Arhat, 'having done all that was to be done,' there is nothing more that should be done, and therefore no possibility of merit or demerit. Injunctions and prohibitions do not have any meaning where there is no longer anything that ought or ought not to be done."[66]

In the Western tradition this point of view did not fail to find recognition. Coomaraswamy refers to Meister Eckhart's statement that neither vice nor virtue can enter into the Kingdom of God, just as in the Upanishads it is said that "neither vice nor virtue can pass over the Bridge of Immortality," and just as the Buddhist idea of the Arhat is of one "no longer under the Law" but a "Mover-at-will" and "Doer of what he will." "If *we* find that he acts unselfishly in our ethical sense of the word, that is our interpretation, for which he is not responsible." Coomaraswamy finds the same point of view expressed in a different way by Nietzsche, who is usually regarded as the most untraditional of thinkers: "The doctrine of the Superman, whose virtue stands 'beyond good and evil,' who is at once the flower and the leader and the savior of men, has been put forward again and again in the world's history. A host of names for this ideal occurs in Indian literature: he is the *Arhat* (adept), *Buddha* (enlightened), *Jina* (conqueror), *Tirthānkara* (finder of the ford), *Bodhisattva* (incarnation of the bestowing virtue) and above all *Jīvan-mukta* (freed in this life), whose actions are no longer good or bad, but proceed from his freed nature."[67]

Coomaraswamy quotes these words from Nietzsche: "That ye

might become weary of saying 'an action is good because it is unselfish.' Ah, my friends! that your very self be in your action, as the mother is in the child: let that be your formula of virtue." And he comments, "This is the very prayer of Socrates, 'and may the outward and inward man be one' — all else is hypocrisy. The inferior man regulates his life by externals ... The superior man is of another sort. Of superior men it can be said, with Chuang Tzu: 'They live in accordance with their own nature. In the whole world they have no equal. They regulate their life by inward things.' "[68] Nietzsche's Superman, who represents the highest attainment and purpose of humanity "is most difficult for self-assertive minds to grasp. A being 'beyond good and evil, a law unto himself! How wicked!' exclaims the ordinary man."[69] This reaction results from the assumption that an action is good only if it is *praiseworthy*. Perfection, however, consists of being detached from praise and blame alike, declares Coomaraswamy. The Superman, acting in accordance with his own nature, becomes utterly spontaneous; and his wisdom is revealed in his refusal to be swayed by pairs of opposites.

CHAPTER 5

The Philosophy of Art

WE have now seen Coomaraswamy's exposition of the metaphysical foundation of the perennial philosophy and the religious and ethical implications resulting from it. We must now turn to the various fields of human life and culture which Coomaraswamy views in the light of this traditional philosophy. In the context of his lifelong study of art, his great experience in handling art objects, and his specialized researches in the history of Hindu and Buddhist art, it is natural that he should have devoted greater attention to the operation of the perennial philosophy in the aesthetic side than in any other side of life. Indeed, even in his discussion of social or educational issues the aesthetic concern is always there in the background.

"It is not the personal view of anyone that I shall try to explain," he says, "but that doctrine of art which is intrinsic to the Philosophia Perennis and can be recognized wherever it has not been forgotten that 'culture' originates in work and not in play."[1] This remark occurs in the very first paragraph of Coomaraswamy's essay entitled *The Christian and Oriental or True Philosophy of Art.* Two points follow from the title itself: first, that he regards the Christian and the oriental attitude to art as essentially the same; and second, that he considers this to be the true (that is universally valid and normal) view of art. When he reminds us that "culture originates in work, not in play," he does not suggest that art is a somber, grim affair but merely that it grows out of actual processes of life and should not be seen as something apart. Coomaraswamy's writings on art show a constant recurrence of this theme. It was his firm conviction that one of the major aberrations of the modern age is the division of life into the "practical" and the "cultural" spheres, and that the imbalance can only be corrected by returning to the orthodox view of culture in general and of art in

95

particular. His exposition of this view carries the stamp of this intensely felt conviction. "I believe what I have to expound," he says at the beginning of the essay referred to above, "for the study of any subject can live only to the extent that the student himself stands or falls by the life of the subject studied; the interdependence of faith and understanding applying as much to the theory of art as to any other doctrine."[2]

I   *A Critique of the Term "Aesthetics"*

The modern view of art is mainly hedonistic. It asserts that while other types of activities serve some practical purposes, art is to be judged solely in terms of the *pleasure* it affords us. Art is not valuable for its role in promoting (or reflecting) the harmony between man and man, or between man and nature; it is valuable for its own sake. This hedonistic view, as we shall presently see, is based upon that individualism of which modern man is so proud. Now since the use of the term *aesthetics* betrays this hedonistic bias, Coomaraswamy is highly critical of this term. He indicates this bias by putting the word in quotation marks so as to demonstrate that he is using it unwillingly. "Our 'aesthetic' appreciation," he says, "is essentially sentimental, because that is just what the word 'aesthetic' means, a kind of feeling rather than an understanding."[3] And again: "Our sentimental or aesthetic culture — sentimental, aesthetic and materialistic are virtually synonyms — prefers instinctive expression to the formal beauty of rational art."[4] He reminds us that "*aisthesis* in Hellenistic usage implies physical affectability as distinguished from mental operations."[5] At one time, Coomaraswamy points out, art was valued for its profound educational value, and "sculpture was thought of as the poor man's 'book.' "[6] But now "our very word 'aesthetics' (from 'aisthesis' or 'feeling') proclaims our dismissal of the intellectual values of art." Art, in fact, was never regarded as "aesthetic activity" until the rise of the materialistic world view upon which modern industrial society is founded. "It is no accident that it should have been discovered only comparatively recently that art is essentially an 'aesthetic' activity," writes Coomaraswamy. "No real distinction can be drawn between aesthetic and materialistic; *aisthesis* being sensation, and matter being that which can be sensed."[7]

This is not a mere matter of usage. The etymology is important because it affects the criteria we adopt. Lest it be objected that

Coomaraswamy was exaggerating, it would be useful to note the background in which Baumgarten first used the term *Aesthetics* to denote the Science of the Beautiful (or the Philosophy of Art, it being assumed that Art is the production of beauty). Philosophers of the Cartesian school, "working downwards" from logical ideas to sense-perception and passion (which Spinoza described as "confused acts of thought") cleared the ground for the study of "sensible" or obscure knowledge as distinct from the analysis of clear knowledge: in other words the study of aesthetics was prefatory to that of logic. The subject of Baumgarten's *Aesthetica* is "obscure knowledge *qua* obscure, that is knowledge in the form of feeling and remaining in that form."[8]

This association of art with sensation or sensibility is reflected in the modern psychologist's interest in the "likes and dislikes" of individuals, their personal preferences, to which is given the dignified name of "aesthetic reactions."[9] In traditional societies — whether advanced or primitive — art was looked upon as something which arose out of the deeper necessities of life itself; therefore it could never have been imagined that the question of "what pleases me, and why?" had any connection with art. Coomaraswamy illustrates this fact by quoting from a recent study of the art of New Guinea: "Aesthetic pathology is an excrescence upon a genuine interest in art which seems to be peculiar to civilized peoples."[10] In view of all this Coomaraswamy suggests that any study of traditional art should begin by discarding the term *aesthetic* altogether.

That is why this chapter has been titled "The Philosophy of Art" rather than "Aesthetics." However, the term has established itself in modern scholarship in the fields of art criticism as well as philosophy, and it is not always possible to discard it. Coomaraswamy has himself used it on many occasions. He speaks of the "aesthetic process" or "aesthetic intuition," and one of his essays bears the title "Aesthetics of the Shukranītisāra." In the paragraphs that follow, I may use the term *aesthetic* here and there in the general sense of "that which is connected with art-creation or art-experience." Such usage is for expediency only, subject to the understanding that Coomaraswamy would prefer avoiding it.

II *Art in an Integrated Society*

This discussion of the term *aesthetics* has prepared us for an examination of the traditional view of art as understood by Coomaraswamy. The outlines of this view may be stated, for the sake of convenience, as follows:

(1) The end of art is "the good of man." This good consists in his spiritual as well as material well-being. Art without use is a luxury, and utility without art is subhuman.

(2) Art is not for mere delectation or pleasurable sensations or feelings. There is no essential difference between the fine arts and the useful arts, or between an artist and a craftsman. Nor is there any basic distinction between classical and popular or folk art.

(3) Self-expression is not the main aim of art in traditional societies. What the artist expresses is not that which is "characteristic" but that which is universal and imperishable. Glorification of, or obsession with, one's own personality is a sign of superficiality in art.

(4) Artistic "freedom" does not mean absence of responsibility or commitment. The true artist reflects and strengthens the harmony between the different sides of human life and between man and nature. Unbridled "freedom" interrupts this harmony.

(5) The value attached to genius, inspiration and originality is in inverse proportion to the true understanding of the purpose and function of art. The artist is not a special kind of man, nor is he entitled to a privileged position superior to that of the workman.

(6) There is no absolute distinction between the religious and the secular in art. Everything in nature and human life is pervaded by the Divine Ground, and all art is religious to some extent. The final goal of art is to reach Divinity. God is the Supreme Artist.

(7) Through contemplation, the artist can visualize Perfection and identify himself with it. Art is Yoga.

(8) Art in the traditional sense is symbolic, not illustrative or historical. Symbols constitute the language of art. Realism or "likeness" is not the primary concern of art. True representation is that of the idea, the form, not of the substance of the perceived object.

(9) Beauty is the "attractive power of perfection." It is objective. It is analogous to truth. It is Reality perceived by the artist.

(10) The essential element in art is the flavor (*rasa*) which determines the aesthetic emotion. This is a transcendental experience and is of the same type as the mystical experience of the Divine.

I will now elaborate Ananda Coomaraswamy's views (or rather his interpretation of traditional views) on art and beauty, taking the points mentioned above as guidelines. As far as possible, I will follow the order in which the issues are listed above and will illustrate them by excerpts from Coomaraswamy's writings. In the remainder of this chapter, all sentences placed within quotation marks are from Coomaraswamy, except where otherwise noted.

III *Purposiveness of Art*

The perennial philosophy assumes that man is a spiritual as well as a psychophysical being. Art justifies itself by fulfilling the needs of both these aspects and does so in a manner which gives us delight. "A need, or 'indigence,' as Plato calls it, is thus the first cause of the production of art."[11] The fashion of regarding art as something "purposeless" is a modern aberration. (Oscar Wilde stated plainly that "all art is utterly useless"; others have been more guarded but *mean* the same thing.) Art is the right or proper way of making things that satisfy man's legitimate needs in a well-adjusted community. "There can be no doubt about the purpose of art in a traditional society: when it has been decided that such and such a thing should be made, it is *by art* that it can be properly made. There can be no good use without art; that is, no good use if things are not properly made,"[12] states Coomaraswamy. Thus, according to the "historically normal and religiously orthodox view," art is "the making well of whatever needs making, just as ethics is the right way of doing things."[13] Man is a doer as well as a maker. He has a soul, an intellect, and a will. A need is felt in the soul, the intellect suggests a solution, the will executes it. This is true of all activities, all vocations — that of the doctor or the priest no less than the sculptor or painter. From this point of view, Coomaraswamy writes, "every activity involves what we now call an aesthetic process, a succession of problem, solution and execution. Materials apart, whoever acts, acts in the same way, will following the intellect."[14] Coomaraswamy attaches great importance to this notion of "vocational making." Each man in traditional society does that kind of work for which he is best fitted by his own nature, "and for which he is therefore destined." "In this way," says Plato, "more will be done, and better done, than in any other way."[15]

This view of art breaks down in industrial societies because an artificial barrier is erected between work (doing what we must, whether we like it or not) and culture (something done or experienced for pure pleasure without reference to any need). "Our hankering for a state of leisure is proof of the fact that most of us are working at a task to which we could never have been called by any one but a salesman, certainly not by God or by our own natures," states Coomaraswamy.[16] Work has been divorced from culture, and culture restricted to something we are supposed to acquire in hours of leisure. "But there can only be an unreal and hothouse culture where work itself is not its means," Coomaraswamy says; "if culture does not show itself in all we make, we are not cultured."[17] Coomaraswamy refers to traditional craftsmen in the East whom he met and who were so deeply attached to their work that they had to be dragged away from it. But in modern industrial society, he says, "we have lost this vocational way of living, the way that Plato made his type of justice." While the modern aesthetician interprets art in terms of pleasure, he continues, the "pleasure afforded by art, whether in the making or in subsequent appreciation, is not enjoyed or even supposed to be enjoyed by the workman at work. The craftsman likes talking about his handicraft. The workman likes talking about the ball game."[18]

In the modern age it is assumed that a man is happy if he can get away from his work and is at play. But it is a cruel error to pretend that the so-called higher things of life can be enjoyed by turning away from one's own vocation. Coomaraswamy quotes from the *Bhagavadgītā:* "The man devoted to his own vocation finds perfection. That man whose prayer and praise of God are in the doing of his own work perfects himself."[19] The dichotomy between work and play leads to the belief that utility and beauty are two different values and that the artist is concerned only with the latter. And this, in turns, leads to the alleged distinction between fine art and useful or decorative art. This entire division was unknown to traditional societies (in which Coomaraswamy includes primitive societies). "Industry without art is brutality. Art is specifically human. None of those primitive peoples, past or present, whose culture we affect to despise, and propose to amend, ever dispensed with art," Coomaraswamy states.[20] In all ancient civilizations, except in periods of decadence, it was assumed that "the human value of anything made is determined by the coincidence in it of beauty and utility, significance and aptitude."[21] And the irony of it is that the artist, whom the modern aesthetician tries to elevate above the workman, suffers as much as the workman does as the result of the dichotomy between art and craft. "The workman loses because he is forced to work unintelligently," Coomaraswamy writes, "goods being valued above men." And the artist loses "by his isolation and corresponding pride, and by the emasculation of his art . . . . which is conceived only as emotional in motivation and significance."[22]

It may be objected that Plato himself speaks disparagingly of the "base mechanical arts" and distinguishes "mere labor" from "fine work." But the objection will be raised only by one who thinks of utility in purely biological terms. What Plato looks down upon is manufacture which caters to the body alone and which, indeed, cannot be called art. "The kind of art which Plato calls wholesome and will admit to his ideal state must be not only useful but also true to rightly chosen models and therefore beautiful, and this art, he says, will provide at the same time 'for the souls and bodies of your citizens.' "[23] writes Coomaraswamy. His "music" stands for cultural and his "gymnastics" for physical well-being; and he insists that these ends of culture and physique should not be separately pursued; "the tender artist and the brutal athlete are equally contemptible," he says.[24]

When, therefore, art is regarded as "making what needs to be made," it must be clearly understood that the need is spiritual as well as physical and mental. "From the stone age onwards, everything made by man, under whatever conditions of hardship or poverty, has been made to serve a double purpose, at once utilitarian and ideological,"[25] says Coomaraswamy. It is only in the modern age that we, who possess more resources than any other society ever had, make a division of art into a part that is barely utilitarian and another part that is luxurious and out of reach of the vast majority. It is becoming increasingly difficult for the modern man to understand "how things made for use can also have a meaning." We separate the functional from the significant, limiting the former to that part of man which is supposed to subsist "by bread alone."[26] As for significant art, it is assumed to be accessible to the fortunate few who can afford it, or have been specially trained to derive pleasure from it. "The insincerity and inconsistency of the whole position is to be seen in the fact that we do not expect of the 'significant' art that it be significant *of* anything, says Coomaraswamy; "If the artist himself declares that his work is charged with meaning, we call it an irrelevance, but decide that he may have been an artist in spite of it. In other words, if the merely functional arts are the husks, the fine arts are the tinsel of life, and art for us has no significance whatever."[27]

IV *Further Comments on Hedonism in Art*

As we have seen from Coomaraswamy's criticism of the word

aesthetics, and from his statement of the traditional view regarding the purposiveness of art, the production of pleasurable feelings or sensations cannot be regarded as the criterion of art. This point occupies such an important place in Coomaraswamy's writings on the subject that it appears appropriate to examine the matter a little further. He states the hedonistic position as follows: "We speak of a work of art as 'felt' and never of its 'truth,' or only of its truth to natural feeling; 'appreciation' is a 'feeling into' the work appreciated. Now, an emotional reaction is evoked by whatever we like or dislike...; what we like we call beautiful, admitting at the same time that matters of taste are not subject to law. The purpose of art is then to reveal a beauty that we like or can be taught to like; the purpose of art is to give pleasure; the work of art as the source of pleasure is its own end; art is for art's sake."[28]

The implication of this view is that the value of an art work lies in its ability to produce the pleasure of sight, sound, or touch. "Our conception of beauty is literally skin-deep; questions of utility and intelligibility rarely arise; and if they arise they are dismissed as irrelevant," says Coomaraswamy. If we try to analyze or "dissect" the pleasure derived from a work of art, says Coomaraswamy, "it becomes a matter of psychoanalysis, and ultimately a sort of science of affections and behaviors."[29] We use high-sounding words like *Empathy* and *Significant Form,* but the use of these words does little or nothing to mitigate our sensationalistic bias. Empathy is nothing but "feeling into"; and as for Significant Form, we ignore the fact that "nothing can properly be called a "sign" that is not significant *of* something other than itself, and for the sake of which it exists."[30] To say that art is essentially a matter of feeling is to say that "its sufficient purpose is to please." The work of art then becomes a luxury, accessory to the life of pleasure. Coomaraswamy is not suggesting that pleasures are "not legitimate." He does say, "But there is a profound distinction between the deliberate pursuit of pleasure and the enjoyment of pleasures proper to the active or contemplative life."[31]

Let us now turn to the views of ancient thinkers on this question. To begin with India, we find that the austerity which marked religious and ethical attitudes in certain periods led to a hedonistic concept of art "on the rebound." That is, instead of saying that "art *should be* for pleasure only" it was asserted that "since art is supposed to be for pleasure only it should be condemned." In the Pali texts of early Buddhism we see this suspicion of art. Coomaraswamy cites a passage from the *Visuddhi Magga:* "Living beings, on account of their love of and devotion to the sensations excited by forms and the other objects of sense, give high honor to painters, musicians, perfumers, cooks, elixir-prescribing physicians, and other like persons who furnish us with objects of sense."[32] In the monastic life of Hinayana Buddhism, there was hardly any place for the arts. Even music was limited to the chanting of the *triratna* ("Three Jewels").[33] In Hinduism, too, this puritanical estimate of art can be seen to persist until the third or second centuries B.C. Manu disapproved of householders singing or dancing, and warned against inviting actors, singers — even architects — to religious ceremonies. Kautilya tolerates musicians and actors, but classes them among courtesans.[34]

Later, however, it was realized that art need not be looked upon as a source of pleasure only, that there is a nobler and more profound role which it can perform. In the classical schools of Indian poetics the hedonistic interpretation of art was abandoned, and the spiritual aspect of aesthetic experience was stressed. In Plato we find both the negative and the positive sides of this attitude. On the one hand he condemns art which caters to man's love of sensation; on the other hand he puts forward the idealistic view which is one of the classic statements of the traditional doctrine of art. Plato asks us "to stand up like men against our instinctive reactions to what is pleasant or unpleasant, and to admire in works of art not their aesthetic surfaces but the right reason for their composition."[35] Whatever is made only to give pleasure is, for Plato, "a mere toy," for the delectation of that part of us which passively submits to emotional storms; "whereas the education to be derived from works of art should be an education in the love of what is ordered and the dislike of what is disordered."[36]

Plato asks of tragic poetry: To what does this wondrous muse devote herself? Is all her aim and desire only to give pleasure to the spectators, or does she fight against and refuse to speak of their pleasant vices, and willingly proclaim in word and song truths welcome and unwelcome? Which is her true character? His answer is that poetry has her face turned towards pleasure and gratification, which is a kind of flattery, an appeasement of the lower side of our nature. This conclusion is obviously very painful to Plato. He *wants* to give poetry a chance to defend herself. "We might allow the lovers and advocates of poetry," he says, "to make what defense they can of her, and to show that she is not only pleasant but also profitable to nations and to mankind. And we shall hear them gladly. For it will be no little gain to us if poetry can be shown to be profitable as well as pleasant.... But if they fail, my dear Glaucon, we shall behave like people who have fallen in love with some one, but do not think that their love can come to any good.... Because of the passion for this poetry which has been bred in us by our national culture, we shall be willing that she should be vindicated as perfectly true and good. But until she can establish her innocence ... we shall whisper to ourselves that we must not take the attractions of such poetry too seriously, as if they had anything to do with truth or goodness; and that her hearer must always mistrust her as an enemy of his soul's peace."[37]

It will be noted that Plato's grievance is against "such poetry," not all poetry; and his comments are equally applicable to the other arts. He condemns the artist *if* he makes the production of pleasurable feelings his sole aim. But in traditional philosophy it is also assumed that great art can be, and has been, produced which does not have this aim. Coomaraswamy gives two examples: Dante and Ashvaghosha. Dante clearly says of his *Divine Comedy* that "the whole work was undertaken for a practical end ... to remove those who are living in this life from the state of wretchedness and to lead them to the state of blessedness."[38] And Ashvaghosha, in the Colophon to his *Saundarananda:* "This poem, pregnant with the burden of Liberation, has been composed by me in the poetic manner, not for the sake of giving pleasure, but for the sake of giving peace, and to win over other-minded hearers. If I have dealt in it with subjects other than that of Liberation, that pertains to what is proper to poetry — to make it tasty, just as when honey is mixed with a medicinal herb ... I have spoken here of the Principle in the garb of poetry, holding that Liberation is the primary value. Whoever understand this, let him retain what is set forth, and not the play of fancy, just as only the gold is cared for when it has been separated from the ore and dross."[39]

To sum up Coomaraswamy's position on this question: Art gives us delight precisely because it fulfills the fundamental needs of our body and soul. It will, as a natural course, give pleasure if "things that need to be made are well made." But pleasure is not its sole aim, not even its primary aim. This is the normal (and also traditional) view of art. "Our modern 'aesthetic' appreciation, essentially sentimental, has nothing to do with the raison d'etre of art," says Coomaraswamy. We derive pleasure from exotic but purposeless works of art "which are not foods but sauces to our palate."[40] If they please our taste, if they become fashionable, it only means that we have over-eaten of unhealthy foods. Coomaraswamy adds: "To 'enjoy' what does not correspond to any vital needs of our own, and what we have not verified in our own life, can only be described as an indulgence."[41] Such indulgence has nothing to do with the deep and profound experience which genuine art is capable of evoking in us.

V *Self Expression, Freedom, Originality*

The traditional philosophy of art can be understood not only by contrasting it with the hedonistic view which, as we have seen, culminates in the dogma of Art for Art's Sake, but also in its rejection of individualism. Indeed, hedonism and individualism are closely related. It is but a short step from "The beautiful is that which gives pleasure" to "The beautiful is that which pleases *me*." Plato's criticism was directed as much against the latter as against the former. The implications of individualism, typical of modern Western civilization, are: that the important thing is for the artist to express himself, his own "personality"; that his aim is therefore to convey what is novel, unique, "original" or "characteristic" rather than what is common to all mankind; and that this demands a complete freedom for the artist, a complete absence of restraint, discipline, or concern for convention. All these ideas are at variance with the traditional stress on harmony, adjustment, proportion, rhythm, and acceptance of universally valid norms.

The distinction between the two points of view may be stated in the words of an outstanding modern writer on aesthetics, Bernard Bosanquet. At the time Bosanquet published his *History of Aesthetic* (1892), the extreme form of individualism with which we are familiar today had not yet arisen. Nevertheless, the shift from the harmonious to the "characteristic" had already been made. "Among the ancients," says Bosanquet, "the fundamental theory of the beautiful was connected with the notions of rhythm, symmetry, harmony of parts; in short, with the general formula of unity in variety. Among the moderns we find that more emphasis is laid on the idea of significance, expressiveness ... in general, that is to say, on the conception of the characteristic.... When with the birth of the modern world the romantic sense of beauty was awakened, accompanied by the craving for free and passionate expression, it became impossible that impartial theory should continue to consider that the beautiful was adequately explained as the regular and harmonious, or as the simple expression of unity in variety."[42]

"The craving for free and passionate expression" which Bosanquet sees as an "accompaniment" of the romantic sense of beauty, gradually became the dominant feature of modern thought. Coomaraswamy examines this feature in detail and shows how it has not only "perverted" the true place of art in human life but has also led to misconceptions regarding ancient and medieval culture. He sometimes uses the word *humanism* in a derogatory sense, suggesting that modern individualism is excessively "man-centered," ignoring not only the transcendental Reality but also the rest of the non-human universe. The following paragraph is representative of Coomaraswamy's estimate of the modern attitude:

Individualists and humanists as we are, we attach an inordinate value to personal opinion and personal experience, and feel an insatiable interest in the personal experience of others. The work of art has come to be, for us, a sort of autobiography of the artist. Art having been abstracted from the general activity of making things for human use, material or spiritual, has come to mean for us the projection in a visible form of the feelings or reactions of the peculiarly-endowed personality of the artist, and especially of those most peculiarly-endowed personalities which we think of as 'inspired' or describe in terms of genius. Because the artistic genius is mysterious we, who accept the humbler status of the workman, have been only too willing to call the artist a 'prophet' and in return for his 'vision' to allow him many privileges that a common man might hesitate to exercise."[43]

The traditional artist, on the other hand, declares Coomaraswamy, "devotes himself to the good of the work to be done." His operation is a rite, "the celebrant neither intentionally nor even consciously expressing himself."[44] Quoting Saint Paul's remark, *Vivo autem jam non ego,* Coomaraswamy points out that works of traditional art (whether oriental, Christian or folk art) are hardly ever signed. Names rarely survive; and if they do survive, very little is known of the men who bore the names. Coomaraswamy adds, "This is true as much for literary as for plastic artifacts. In traditional arts it is never 'Who said?' but only 'What was said?' that concerns us: for 'all that is true, by whomsoever it has been said, has its origin in the Spirit.' "[45] This anonymity is directly related to the metaphysical concept of the Self. The self-effacement of the artist "belongs to a type of culture dominated by the longing to be liberated from oneself. All the force of this philosophy is directed against the delusion: 'I am the doer,' 'I' am not in fact the doer, but the instrument; human individuality is not an end but only a means.''[46] Coomaraswamy refers to all the three religious traditions — Christian, Hindu, and Buddhist — in support of this view. Christ said: "I do nothing of myself." In the *Bhagavad-gītā*, Krishna declares that "the Comprehensor cannot form the concept 'I am the doer.' " And in the *Dhammapada* we are told: "To wish that it may be known that 'I was the author' is the thought of a person not yet adult."

When, therefore, it is said that "Art is Expression," it is important to determine *what* is expressed. The traditional artist does not express himself but only a thesis. Coomaraswamy writes, "Both human and divine art are expressions, but only to be spoken of as 'self-expressions' if it has been clearly understood what 'self' is meant."[47] Failure to grasp this has led many modern scholars to misunderstand, and sometimes to denigrate, traditional art. Histories of art are studied in terms of style sequences. But "styles are the accident and by no means the essence of art." It is emphasized only when art is attributed to individual idiosyncracies, which are reflected in stylistic peculiarities. Coomaraswamy writes, "Our conception of art as essentially the expression of a personality, our impertinent curiosities about the artist's private life, all these are the products of a perverted individualism and prevent our understanding of the true nature of medieval and oriental art. The modern mania for attribution is the expression of Renaissance conceit and nineteenth century humanism; it has nothing to do with the nature of medieval art, and it becomes a pathetic fallacy when applied to it."[48]

What is so fondly praised as "free thought" really turns out to be a prop for individualism. The much-vaunted "freedom to think for oneself" becomes the "freedom to think *of* oneself."[49] And that is really no freedom at all because we are dependent upon those very desires and thoughts of the self for which we are claiming the right of expression. "Free thought is a passion; it is much rather the thoughts than ourselves that are free," says Coomaraswamy. Does this mean that the perennial philosophy attaches no importance to freedom in the domain of artistic creation? Not at all, says Coomaraswamy. Plato describes "bad art" as "unworthy of free men." The artist, however, is also a *man* and is responsible to the community in which he lives. Above all he is responsible to the highest truth which is the foundation of everything specifically human, including freedom. To put it negatively, the artist is not free to ignore truth, assuming that he has freely given his assent to it. ·

The traditional philosophy of art makes no attempt to conceal the assumption that the artist must conform to the metaphysical basis of life and to the conventions evolved through centuries of experience as to the best manner in which he can fulfill his vocation. It may be asked, how can he be described as free if he is working to a formula? The answer is that working to a formula can either be mechanical or joyous and spontaneous. In quantitative production work becomes mechanical, and therefore the craftsman who blindly copies the model is indeed not free. Coomaraswamy says, "It would be the same in the performance of any rite, to the extent that performance becomes a habit, unenlivened by any recollection."[50] The mechanical product may still turn out to be a work of art; "but the art was not the workman's, nor the workman an artist, but a hireling."[51] This situation, however, is far more common in the modern industrial society than it was in traditional societies.

This entire question of freedom involves a discussion of what the artist is trying to "imitate." As we shall presently see, the orthodox view is that the artist expresses "primordial forms." The highest "form" is the supreme truth which is identical with his own innermost Self. In all creative ages it has been assumed that the artist does not blindly copy anything extrinsic but expresses that which is the most essential part of himself, even when he adheres to a "conventional prescription" or even if he responds to requirements that may remain unchanged for thousands of years. Therefore, to say that "art has fixed ends and ascertained means of operation," as Thomas Aquinas put it, is not to deny the artist's freedom. Coomaraswamy says, "It is only the academician and the hireling whose work is under constraint. It is true that if the artist has not conformed *himself* to the 'form' of the thing to be made, he has not really known it and cannot work originally. But if he *has* thus conformed himself, he will be in fact expressing *himself* in bringing it forth."[52] Clearly, then, the traditional view of the artist's freedom is intelligible in terms of its religious foundation. It is unintelligible only in a society where there is no place for the trans-human in human affairs.

The artist, in order to be free "does not have to express his 'personality,' himself as 'this man,' 'So-and-So,' but himself *sub specie aeternitatis,* and apart from individual idiosyncracy," declares Coomaraswamy. "The idea of the thing to be made is brought to life in him, and it will be from this supra-individual life of the artist himself that the vitality of the finished work will be derived."[53] In such a view "originality" or "the characteristic" is not lauded for its own sake, as it is fashionable to do in our age. "To idolize one who is still a man as something more than man, to glorify rebellion and independence, as in the modern deification of genius and tolerance of the vagaries of genius"[54] would appear preposterous to any one genuinely concerned with that perfection without which there is no true freedom, says Coomaraswamy. "The way to liberty has nothing in common with willful rebellion or calculated originality." What is praised as *originality* is often only *novelty,* and the craving to be novel or different is merely another aspect of individualism. Perhaps there is greater variety in individualistic art than there is in orthodox art. But, while conceding this, Coomaraswamy points out that the high value placed upon variety is the result of the modern man's inability to grasp that there can be, a "unanimous style" reflecting a universally valid philosophy, which can retain its power and vitality for millenia.[55] Just as energy is often mistaken for intensity, so also novelty is often sanctified with the impressive name of originality. "But when there is *realization,* when the themes are *felt* and art *lives,* it is of no moment whether the themes are new or old,"[56] states Coomaraswamy.

This is not to deny the importance of originality in art. Where the artist has identified himself with the idea to be expressed, he works spontaneously and therefore, since diversity is a fact of human nature, it is inevitable that each artist will express the central idea in his own way, says Coomaraswamy. "The primary necessity is that he should really have entertained the idea and always visualized it in a communicable form; and this, implying an intellectual activity that must be ever renewed, is what we mean by originality as distinguished from novelty, and power as distinguished from violence."[57] In short, under the attractive label of "freshness" or "uniqueness," what lies hidden is an extremely superficial approach to the artist as well as his work. "In concentrating our attention on the stylistic peculiarities of works of art, we are confining it to a consideration of accidents, and really only amusing ourselves with a psychological analysis of personalities, not by any means penetrat-

ing to what is constant and essential in the art itself,"[58] writes
Coomaraswamy.

A glance at traditional art through the centuries shows us that it
is continuous, but not repetitive. The continuity is ensured by the
metaphysical foundation on which traditional society is based.
"But nothing can be known or stated except in some way, the way
of the individual knower. Whatever may be known to you and me
in common can only be stated by either of us each in his own
way,"[59] says Coomaraswamy. And along with ways of knowing the
idiom of expression also varies, he adds. "An iconography may not
vary for millenia, and yet the style of every century may be distinct
and recognizable at a glance."[60] Coomaraswamy explains this by
comparing the artist with the orator: "The orator whose sermon is
not the expression of a private opinion or philosophy, but the
exposition of a traditional doctrine, is speaking with perfect freedom and originality; the doctrine is his, not as having invented it,
but by conformation (*adequatio rei et intellectus*). Even in direct
citation he is not a parrot, but giving out of himself a recreated
theme."[61]

The artist works in the service of what he believes in, and "service is perfect freedom." It is only lip-service that is slavish, not service based on faith, Coomaraswamy declares. "When an inherited
formula becomes an 'art form' or an 'ornament,' to be imitated as
such without any understanding of its significance, only then does
the artist — no longer a traditional craftsman but an academician
— become a plagiarist."[62] As examples of plagiarism and complete
absence of originality Coomaraswamy mentions the repetition of
classic forms in modern architecture and the manufacture of
"brummagen idols":[63] "But the hereditary craftsman, who may be
repeating formulae inherited from the stone age, remains an original artist until he is forced by economic pressure to accept the
status of a parasite supplying the demand of the ignorant tourist in
search of drawing-room ornaments."[64] In all traditional cultures —
Indian, Chinese, Hellenic, medieval European — the yearning for
innovation was considered to be a sign of immaturity. Coomaraswamy points out the significant fact that Plato did not admire
what is known as the "Greek miracle." What he praised was the
canonical art of Egypt in which "those modes of representation
that are by nature correct have been held for ever sacred."[65]

But perhaps the most unfortunate illusion generated by individualism is the notion that art is something to be done by a special

kind of man, and particularly that kind of man whom we call a genius. Coomaraswamy states, "The normal view assumes that the artist is not a special kind of man, but that every man who is not a mere idler or a parasite is necessarily some special kind of artist, skilled and well-contented in the making or arranging of one thing or another according to his constitution and training."[66] The genius is supposed to be doubly special — first as an artist, and then as a "special kind of artist" who must be peculiar if he has to live up to his reputation. "Genius inhabits a world of his own. The master craftsman lives in a world inhabited by other men. He has neighbors," says Coomaraswamy.[67] According to the traditional view the important thing is not that the artist should be a genius, that he should be strange or unpredictable, but that he should produce a masterpiece. And even the word *masterpiece,* Coomaraswamy reminds us, has a different meaning in the traditional vocabulary than it has in ours: "A masterpiece is not, as commonly supposed, an individual flight of imagination, beyond the common reach in its own time and place, and rather for posterity than for ourselves; but by definition a masterpiece is a piece of work done by an apprentice at the close of his apprenticeship and by which he proves his right to be admitted into full membership of a guild as a master workman. The masterpiece is simply the proof of competence expected and demanded from every graduate artist.... The man whose masterpiece has thus been accepted by a body of practicing experts is expected to go on producing works of like quality for the rest of his life. He is a man responsible for everything he makes."[68]

With regard to the concepts of genius and inspiration, as in the case of masterpiece, Coomaraswamy reminds us of the original meanings of the words in order to bring out the difference between the traditional and the individualistic views of art. He cites Saint Augustine's usage: "Thou madest that *ingenium* whereby the artificer may take his art, and may see within what he has to do without," and comments: "What Augustine calls *ingenium* corresponds to Philo's *Hegemon,* the Sanskrit 'Inner Controller,' and what is called in medieval theology Synteresis, the Immanent Spirit thought of equally as the artistic, moral and speculative conscience."[69] Thus *ingenium* has nothing to do with what the word *genius* conveys today and is more like the Greek *daimon,* says Coomaraswamy. "No man, considered as So-and-So, can *be* a genius: but all men *have* a genius."[70] While we think of "genius" as a peculiarly developed personality, traditional philosophy sees

the Immanent Spirit, "beside which the individual personality is
relatively nil."[71] As for "inspiration," we nowadays speak of an
artist being inspired by something external to him: a person or an
object. But in the traditional sense, says Coomaraswamy, "inspiration can never mean anything but the working of some spiritual
force within you."[72] Even Webster's dictionary defines it as
"supernatural divine influence." A rationalist may wish to deny
the possibility of inspiration, says Coomaraswamy, "but he must
not obscure the fact that from Homer onwards the word has always
been used with one exact meaning — that of Dante, when he says
that Love, that is to say the Holy Ghost, 'inspires' him, and that he
goes 'setting the matter forth even as He dictates within me.'"[73]

VI   *The Human and the Divine: Art as Yoga*

From the foregoing discussion it should have become apparent,
in various contexts, that in the traditional world view there can be
no dichotomy between religious and secular art. The artist imitates
eternal realities, not the vagaries of human character. His aim is to
grasp the primordial truth, to reproduce primordial images, to
make the inaudible audible. In his interaction with the world of
manifestation, the traditional artist is conscious of the Divine
Ground. The needs which art fulfills are spiritual no less than material: indeed, even the latter subserve the former, "as the lower
always subserves the higher." Plato says that the contemplation
and understanding of works of art can enable us to "attune our
own distorted modes of thought to cosmic harmonies."[74] In India,
the doctrine that human works of art (*shilpāni*) are imitations of
heavenly forms, and that by means of their rhythm a metrical re-
constitution (*samskarana*) of our limited human personality can be
effected, goes back to the period of the Brahmanas.[75] Going further back, we find that primitive man made no sharp distinction
between the sacred and the secular. All the things of daily use — his
weapons, vehicles, houses, utensils, even clothes — were regarded
as imitations of divine prototypes. He "made them more" by
incantation and rites.[76]

The limitations of the human mind and imagination alike make it
inevitable that the Absolute, though impersonal and quality-less in
its essence, should be conceived as the personal God to whom attributes are ascribed. The One who is the creator, sustainer, and
destroyer of the phenomenal universes, the Personal God who is

Supreme Consciousness and Bliss, is in turn viewed by the artist (as by the devotee) in many forms. The metaphor of God as the Supreme Artist and the human artist as being only His instrument recurs in Indian poetry in every age from the *Bhagavadgītā* to Rabindranath Tagore. The same metaphor occurs in the Christian scholastic tradition, as Coomaraswamy shows through citations from Thomas Aquinas and Meister Eckhart. Not only in poetry and iconography, but also in music, it is assumed that the expression of transient or fleeting experience can have no appeal unless it gives a glimpse of the Eternal. Coomaraswamy quotes from Shankaracharya: "Those who sing here, sing God," and from the *Vishnu Purāna:* "All songs are a part of Him who wears a form of sound."[77]

In India, this idea has been made intelligible to the common man through mythology, epic poetry, romances and even ballads. "Sarasvatī, the goddess of speech and learning, or Nārada, whose mission it is to disseminate occult knowledge through the sounds of the *vina's* strings, or Krishna, whose flute is for ever calling us to leave worldly concerns and follow Him — it is these, rather than any human individuals, who speak through the singer's voice, and are seen in the movements of the dancer," writes Coomaraswamy.[78] The heroes of epics and romances are described by modern criticism as "unreal types," which cannot be subjected to psychological analysis,[79] much to the critic's disappointment. The modern critic fails to appreciate, Coomaraswamy writes, that "the romance is still essentially an epic, and the epic essentially a myth; and that it is just because the hero exhibits universal qualities, without individual peculiarity or limitation, that he can be an imitable pattern.... In the last analysis, the hero is always God, whose only idiosyncrasy is being, and to whom it would be absurd to attribute individual characteristics."[80] In trying to secularize the myths, and to humanize the mythical heroes and heroines by speaking of them as though they were personalities, we flatter ourselves that we are providing a "realistic corrective." Actually we are simply missing the point behind the entire tradition of myth-making.

The seriousness with which the religious import is taken by the traditional artist can be seen by the preparation which he makes before undertaking his work. "The Indian actor prepares for his performance by prayer," writes Coomaraswamy. "The Indian architect is often spoken of as visiting heaven and there making notes of the prevailing forms of architecture which he imitates here below."[81] As for the sculptor, ancient Hindu texts give details of the kind of man who is qualified to make images of the gods. Here is one passage quoted by Coomaraswamy: "The Shilpan (artificer) should understand the Atharva Veda, the thrity-two Shilpa Shāstras, and the Vedic *mantras* by which the deities are invoked. He should wear a sacred thread, a necklace of holy beads, and a ring of *kusha* grass on his finger; delighting in the worship of God, faithful to his wife, piously acquiring a knowledge of various sciences. Such a one is indeed a craftsman."[82] In another text, the moral and spiritual prerequisites of a painter are thus described: "The painter must be a good man, no sluggard, not given to anger; holy, learned, self-controlled, devout and charitable — such should be his character."[83] The artist who possessed these qualifications was assured of his high status and received state protection from competition and undercutting. To allow any one but a craftsman, any one who was not properly trained and did not possess the appropriate moral and spiritual qualities, to build a temple, a tank, or even a well, was regarded as a grievous sin.[84]

Let us now see how the traditional artist proceeds in his search for the Divine. Many steps are involved: contemplation, visualization of the ideal forms, identification with the form visualized, and communication. We can observe these steps with particular reference to the work of the image-maker, it being understood that the basic procedure is the same in other arts as well. Coomaraswamy's account, based on Buddhist texts, is paraphrased below. The maker of an icon, having by various means eliminated the distracting influences of fugitive emotions, having set aside self-willing and self-thinking, proceeds to visualize the form of the *devatā* (an aspect of God) as described in a given canonical prescription. As Coomaraswamy writes, "The mind 'pro-duces' or 'draws' (*ākar-shati*) this form to itself, as though from a great distance: ultimately, that is, from Heaven, where the types of art exist in formal operation; and immediately from the 'immanent space in his heart' (*antar-hridaya-ākāsha*), the common focus of seer and seen, at which place the only possible experience of reality takes place. The true-knowledge-purity-aspect (*jñāna-sattva-rupa*) thus conceived and inwardly known (*antar-jneya*) reveals itself against the ideal space (*ākāsha*) like a reflection (*pratibimbavat*), or as if seen in a dream (*svapnavat*)."[85]

Such a visualization, resulting in the "appearance" of the ideal form, demands concentration of a special type. In describing this concentration of the artist Indian writers frequently employ the vocabulary of Yoga. Coomaraswamy refers to Kālidāsa's play, *Mālavikāgnimitra,* where a painter, who has missed the beauty of his model, attributes his failure to imperfect absorption (*shithila samādhi*) rather than want of observation.[86] A similar reference is found in the *Shukranītisāra,* where it is said that even when a horse is to be modelled, the work should commence with deep concentration (*dhyātvā kuryat*).[87] *Dhyāna* and *samādhi* are terms used by Patanjali, the founder of the classical system of Yoga, to denote concentration and absorption respectively.[88] Coomaraswamy points out that the idea of art as Yoga is implicit in the word *shruti* applied to the Vedas. As differentiated from *smriti* ("remembered"), Vedic wisdom is said to be *shruti* ("heard"). "This is not a theory of 'revelation' in the ordinary sense," declares Coomaraswamy "since the audition depends on the qualification of the hearer, not on the will and active manifestation of a god."[89] Just as the qualified sage "hears" God, so also the qualified artist sees God through Yogic absorption. The idea of art as Yoga is important for an understanding of the traditional view of art and deserves some further discussion here.

The purpose of Yoga is mental concentration, carried to a point where the distinction between the subject and the object of contemplation is transcended and the harmony (or unity) of consciousness is achieved. It is realized by many ancient writers on aesthetics that the concentration of the artist is of the same kind. Even lesser crafts, like arrow-making, involve a practice analogous to Yoga. In the Bhāgavata Purāna we find this sentence: "I have learnt concentration from the maker of arrows." And Shankarāchārya, explaining the distinction between Yogic absorption and "swooning," says, "The arrow-maker perceives nothing beyond his work when he is buried in it; nevertheless he has consciousness and control over his body, both of which are absent in the man who faints."[90] In the higher arts, like that of sculpture, the role of Yogic concentration is even more important. Coomaraswamy quotes from Shukrāchārya: "Let the imager establish images in temples by meditation on the deities who are the objects of his devotion. For the successful achievement of this Yoga, the lineaments of the image are described.... In no other way, not even by direct and immediate vision of an actual object, is it possible to be so absorbed in contemplation, as thus in the making of images."[91]

When it is asserted that even the direct, sensory perception of an object is not as clear as the vision of an ideal form through Yogic concentration, the implication is that there is a way of seeing other than that in which the corporeal eye is used. This is "seeing by identification." "The imager must realize a complete self-identification with the object (the ideal form) whatever its peculiarities, even in the case of opposite sex," says Coomaraswamy, "or even if the divinity is provided with terrible supernatural characteristics. The form thus known in an act of non-differentiation, being held in view as long as may be necessary, is the model from which he proceeds to execute in stone, pigment or other material."[92] In the West, too, similar descriptions of aesthetic vision have been given, though the details were not worked out as meticulously as in Yoga. "Here, indeed," says Coomaraswamy, "European and Asiatic art meet on common ground; according to Eckhart, the skilled painter shows his art, but it is not himself that he reveals to us; and in the words of Dante, 'Who paints a figure, if he cannot be it, cannot draw it.' "[93]

The artist, then, is requried to *be* what he represents. And this is what makes art a religious activity. "The practice of visualization is identical in worship and in art," says Coomaraswamy. "The worshipper recites the *dhyana mantram* describing the deity, and forms a corresponding mental picture; and it is then to this imagined form that his prayers are addressed and the offerings are made. The artist follows identical prescriptions, but proceeds to represent the mental picture in a visible and objective form, by drawing or modelling."[94] An example from a Buddhist text will clarify this. The artist is here referred to as a "realizer" (sādhaka) or a *yogin.* He is asked to proceed to a solitary place after ceremonial purification. He must then perform the "sevenfold office," beginning with the invocation of the hosts of Buddhas and Bodhisattvas, and offering them flowers (real or imaginary). He should then realize in thought the four infinite moods of friendliness, compassion, sympathy, and impartiality. He should meditate upon the emptiness (*Shūnyatā*) or nonexistence of all things, because "by the fire of the idea of the Abyss, the five factors of ego-consciousness (*skandhas*) are destroyed beyond recovery." "Then only should he invoke the desired divinity by uttering the appropriate seedword (*bīja*) and should identify himself completely with the divinity to be represented. Then finally, on pronouncing the *dhyana mantram,* in which the attributes are defined, the divinity appears visibly, like a reflection, and this brilliant image is the artist's model.[95]

This conception of art as Yoga has its parallels in literature as well. It is said that Vālmīki, though perfectly familiar with the story of Rāma, practiced contemplation in order to realize it more profoundly before starting the composition of his *Rāmāyana*. Coomaraswamy quotes from the *Dasharūpa:* "Seating himself with his face towards the East, and sipping water according to rule (i.e., ceremonial purification), he set himself to yoga-contemplation of his theme. By virtue of his yoga-power he saw clearly before him Rāma, Lakshmana, Sītā and Dasharatha ... talking, acting and moving as if in real life.... By yoga-power that righteous one (i.e., Vālmīki) beheld all that had come to pass, and all that was to happen in the future, like a *nelli* fruit on the palm of his hand. And having truly seen everything by his concentration, the generous sage began the setting forth of the history of Rāma."[96]

Coomaraswamy refers to two modern Western thinkers who have put forward similar views on the artist's intuitive knowledge of the very essence of his theme: Jung and Croce. The preparatory concentration described in the Buddhist and Hindu texts quoted above is what Jung calls "the willed introversion of a creative mind which ... inwardly collecting its forces, dips for a moment into the source of life, in order there to wrest a little more strength from the mother for the completion of its work."[97] And Croce's view that "to intuit *is* to express" is in harmony with the description of Vālmīki's visualization of *Rāmayāna* quoted above. "Croce is entirely correct," says Coomaraswamy, "when he speaks of the artist 'who never makes a stroke with his brush without having previously seen it with his imagination,' and remarks that the externalization of a work of art 'implies a vigilant will, which persists in not allowing certain visions, intuitions, or representations to be lost.' "[98] The same idea is suggested by Chuang Tzu when he says, "The mind of the sage, being in repose, becomes the mirror of the universe, the speculum of all creation." The work of art is already completed — the universe is already mirrored in the illumined mind — before the actual work of transcribing, composing, or sketching has even begun.

For the artist, however, Yoga is a means, not the end. Through Yogic concentration he receives the right image of the Divine and fashions it in stone. But he does so *not* for pleasure (therefore not for aesthetic reasons, taking the word *aesthetic* in its original sense), not even to create something beautiful, but simply because that is his way of expressing and satisfying his own religious yearn-

ing and, indirectly, the yearning of others. "As in medieval Europe,
so too, and perhaps even more conspicuously in India," writes
Coomaraswamy, "the impulse to iconolatry derived from the spirit
of adoration: the loving and passionate devotion to a personal
divinity, which we know as *bhakti*."⁹⁹ It should be noted here that
in Patanjali's classic statement of Yoga, based as it is on Sāmkhya
metaphysics, God does not play an important role. God, or Lord,
is only one of the focal points of concentration mentioned by
Patanjali. But when it is said that "Art is Yoga," it is the Yoga of
the theistic *Bhagavadgītā* rather than of the nontheistic Raja Yoga
that is indicated. The psychology of classical Samkhya-Yoga and of
early Buddhism and the somewhat cold metaphysics of Vedanta
appeal more to the intellectual than to the religious or aesthetic
temper. According to Coomaraswamy, "It was the spirit of worship which built upon the foundations of Buddhist and Vedantic
thought the mansions of Indian religion, which shelter all those
whom the purely intellectual formulae could not satisfy — the children of this world who will not hurry along the path of Release,
and the mystics who find a foretaste of freedom in the love of every
cloud in the sky and every flower at their feet."¹⁰⁰

VII   *Symbolism in Traditional Art*

Such being the attitude of the perennial philosophy towards the
creation and enjoyment of art, it is obvious that when the traditional artist or philosopher of art speaks of "imitation" he is thinking of the "imitation of Divine forms" rather than the photographic reproduction of objects or persons out there in the world.
It is the failure to grasp this fact that is responsible for the misinter-
pretations to which the Platonic view of art has been subjected, and
for the praise lavished upon Indian painting *merely* for the accu-
racy and realism with which flowers or birds are delineated. Traditional art certainly does not exclude the representation of actual
objects in all their relationships in the external world or the narration of events and episodes through color and form. But its primary
aim is neither illustrative nor historical.

Coomaraswamy quotes an early text, the *Aitareya Brāhmana*,
regarding the ideal derivation of the types represented by the
human artists: "It is in imitation (*anukriti*) of the angelic (*deva*)
works of art (*shilpāni*) that any work of art (*shilpa*) is accomplished
(*adhigamyate*) here; for example a clay elephant, a brazen object, a

garment, a gold object, and a mule-chariot are 'works of art.' A work of art (*shilpa*), indeed, is accomplished in him who comprehends this. For these angelic works of art (*shilpāni*) are an integration of the Self (*ātma-samskriti*); and by them the sacrificer likewise integrates himself (*ātmānam samskurute*) in the mode of rhythm (*chhandomaya*)."[101] A Reference is also made to the assertion in the Shaiva *Agamas* that the architecture of earthly temples is "Kailāsabhāvana," that is modelled on the forms prevailing in Kailāsa.[102] Coomaraswamy makes it clear, however, that this view cannot be described as "idealistic" in the superficial sense of the term. When realism is rejected, one tends to think of idealism. But, says Coomaraswamy, "we should err equally in supposing that Asiatic art represents an 'ideal' world, a world 'idealized' in the popular (sentimental, religious) sense, that is perfected or remolded near to the heart's desire."[103]

In Indian aesthetics the word *sādrishya* is often used, and this has led to a misunderstanding because *sādrishya* is often translated as "likeness." Though this rendering may be etymologically correct, in the context of art it really implies "correspondence of the formal and representative elements." "That aesthetic *sādrishya* does not imply naturalism, verisimilitude, illustration or illusion in any superficial sense is sufficiently shown by the fact that in Indian lists of factors essential to painting it is almost always mentioned with *pramāna,* 'criterion of truth,' here 'ideal proportion'; and in the Indian theory of knowledge empirical observation (*pratyaksha*), as supplying only a test, and not the material of theory is regarded as the least valid of the various *pramānas*," states Coomaraswamy.[104] *Sādrishya* (literally, "likeness") and *pramāna* ("ideal proportion") only *seem* to be mutually contradictory. But in Indian aesthetics "ideal form and natural shape, although distinct in principle, were not conceived as incommensurable, but rather as coincident in the common unity of the symbol."[105]

Traditional art, then, cannot be described either as idealistic or as naturalistic in the popular sense of these terms. It is "like nature (*natura naturans*) not in appearance (viz., that of *ens naturata*), but in operation."[106] Sādrishya, literally "visual correspondence," is misinterpreted as "having to do with two appearances, that of the work of art and that of the model," says Coomaraswamy. "It refers, actually, to a quality wholly self-contained within the work of art itself, a correspondence of mental and sensational factors in work."[107] Coomaraswamy refers in this context to the *Kaushitakī*

Upanishad, where the sensational and intelligible (formal) aspects of appearance are distinguished as *bhūta-mātrā* and *prajñā-mātrā,* and it is asserted that "truly, from either alone, no aspect (*rupa*) whatsoever would be produced."[108] He explains *sadrishya* as "similitude, but rather such as is implied by 'simile' than by 'simulacrum' "; and adds: "The likeness between anything and any representation of it cannot be a likeness of nature, but must be analogical, or exemplary, or both of these. What the representation imitates is the idea or the species of the thing ... rather than its substance as perceived by the senses."[109]

This explains the important part which symbolism plays in traditional — especially Indian — art. The symbol is employed for imitating the idea. When an Indian deity is represented as having many arms, with total indifference to the demands of realism, the functions associated with that deity are expressed through the objects carried by the various hands. The icon, whether carved or painted, is not just a memory image. It is a visual symbol, says Coomaraswamy. "The Indian icon fills the whole field of vision at once, all is equally clear and equally essential. The eye is not made to range from one point to another, as in empirical vision.... The parts of the icon are not organically related, for it is not contemplated that they should function biologically, but ideally related, being the required component parts of a given type of activity stated in terms of the visible and tangible medium. This does not mean that the various parts are not related, or that the whole is not a unity, but that the relation is mental rather than functional."[110] Pointing out the difference between the modern Western and the traditional oriental approach to this question, Coomaraswamy says, "In Western art the picture is generally conceived as seen in a frame or through a window; but the oriental image really exists only in our own mind and is thence projected or reflected onto space."[111]

Islamic art, Coomaraswamy asserts, is in conformity with the oriental tradition, though its strong opposition to iconography might lead to a different impression. The divergence between Islamic and Indian art is not so much in fundamental principles as in literal interpretation. "Naturalism is antipathetic to religious art of all kinds, ... and the *spirit* of the traditional Islamic interdiction of the representation of living forms is not really infringed by such ideal representations as are met with in Indian or Christian iconography. The Muhammadan interdiction refers to such naturalistic representations as could theoretically, at the Judgment Day, function biologically. But the Indian icon is not constructed as though to function biologically, the Christian icon cannot be thought of as being moved by any other thing than its form, and each should, strictly speaking, be regarded as a kind of diagram, expressing certain ideas, and not as the likeness of anything on earth."[112]

In the light of this discussion, the oriental conception of beauty can also be easily understood. Beauty is not that which pleases me. It is inherent in Reality itself and can be described simply as "the attractive power of Perfection."[113] Beauty is Reality as perceived by the artist, just as truth is Reality as perceived by the philosopher or the sage.[114] It does not arise from the subject of a work of art, but from the inward necessity that has been felt of representing that subject.[115] Beauty is objective, "residing in the artifact and not in the spectator." There can be no "degrees" of beauty, since it is a state, says Coomaraswamy. "The most complex and the simplest expressions remind us of one and the same state. The sonata cannot be more beautiful than the simplest lyric, nor the painting than the drawing, merely because of their greater elaboration." Coomaraswamy takes an analogy from mathematics to illustrate this point. We may consider large and small circles; "they differ only in their content, not in their circularity."[116] Similarly, there are perfections or beauties of different kinds of things, or in different contexts, but we cannot arrange these beauties in a hierarchy.

One of the implications of this view, Coomaraswamy points out, is that the artist's aim is not the discovery or the creation of beauty at all. "Whatever is well and truly made will be beautiful in kind because of its perfection."[117] The artist is always working for the good of the work to be done. "From the coincidence of beauty with perfection it follows inevitably," says Coomaraswamy, "that his operation always tends to the production of a beautiful work. But this is a very different matter from saying that the artist has always in view to discover and communicate beauty... Beauty in the master-craftsman's atelier is not a final cause of the work to be done but an inevitable accident."[118]

VIII   *Beauty as "Rasa"*

I will conclude this study of Coomaraswamy's view of art with a brief reference to the theory of *rasa* in classical Indian poetics. In the concept of *rasa* Coomaraswamy sees the most satisfying expression of the traditional attitude to art. The word *rasa* has been variously rendered as "flavor," "mood," or "aesthetic delight." In Coomaraswamy's terminology, however, *rasa* is *beauty,* and *rasāsvādana* (tasting of *rasa*) is the vision (or experience) of beauty, or aesthetic contemplation. *Rasavanta* (possessing *rasa*), the adjective derived from *rasa,* and *rasika* (one who enjoys *rasa*), all point to a kind of experience which is unique and yet altogether universal. For more than two thousand years Indian commentators have discussed the details regarding the various factors which, in their combination, give rise to *rasa:* the master-motif (sthāyībhāva), the transient feelings (anubhāva), the determinants (vibhāva) and so on. There have also been endless controversies regarding the types into which *rasa* can be classified. But the core of the theory, Coomaraswamy points out, is beyond controversy. It is the identification of aesthetic with religious experience; and this is just what one might expect from the traditional Indian view. *Rasas,* taken in the plural, refer to the permanent moods with which they are associated, usually classified into nine types. But *rasa* itself is an absolute. "The 'nine rasas' are no more than the colorings of one experience, and are arbitrary terms of rhetoric used only for convenience in classification: just as we speak of poetry categorically as lyric, epic, dramatic, etc. without implying that poetry is anything but poetry," declares Coomaraswamy.[119]

This one experience, at its climactic point, is in no way different from the sense of certitude and vividness which the seeker of God has in moments of insight. It is transcendental, wholly unlike any other type of experience, and is — to use a Kantian phrase — "disinterested," that is unconcerned with functional or ethical criteria. "It cannot be an object of knowledge, its perception being indivisible from its very existence," says Coomaraswamy.[120] Apart from perception *rasa* is a mere abstraction. And yet it is timeless, supersensuous, other-worldly (*alaukika*). In our attempts to describe it, we find ourselves employing apparently contradictory epithets, as the sages of the Upanishads did when they tried to communicate the nature of Brahman-Atman. The only proof of its existence is that it compels us to exclaim: "It is." Coomaraswamy quotes a passage from Vishvanatha's *Sāhitya Darpana:* "*Rasa* is pure, indivisible, self-manifested, compounded equally of joy and consciousness, free of admixture with any other perception, the very twin-brother of mystic experience (*Brahmasvadana sahodarah*), and the very life of it is supersensuous (*lokottara*) wonder."

Further, "it is enjoyed by those who are competent thereto, in identity, just as the form of God is itself the joy with which it is recognized."[121]

And so we come back to the conviction which we found to be at the very root of the perennial philosophy: "religion and art are names for one and the same experience — an intuition of reality and of identity."[122]

CHAPTER 6

Society, State, and Education

THE basic tenets of the perennial philosophy are, according to Coomaraswamy, fully applicable to the practical problems of communal life. He points to traditional Indian society as the classic example of an organization based on clear-cut metaphysical and ethical assumptions. In his exposition of social, political, and educational views he draws mainly upon Indian sources. References to the Platonic or the Christian Scholastic points of view are seen in some of Coomaraswamy's essays even on social questions. But such references are much fewer than in his writings on art. While emphasizing that all traditional societies derive their strength from the perennial philosophy, Coomaraswamy sees in the history of Indian culture a clearer and a more persistent confirmation of this connection than in any other culture.

In his essay "What Has India Contributed to Human Welfare?" Coomaraswamy says: "If it be asked what inner riches India brings to aid in the realization of a civilization of the world, then . . . the answer must be found in her religions and her philosophy, and her *constant application of abstract theory to practical life.*"[1] The solutions offered by India, he concedes, cannot be directly applied to modern conditions. "But what I do suggest," he adds, "is that the Hindus grasped more firmly than others the fundamental meaning and purpose of life, and more deliberately than others organized society with a view to the attainment of the fruits of life."[2] Coomaraswamy asserts that Hindu society, in spite of all its imperfections, is "superior to any form of social organization attained on a large scale anywhere else, and infinitely superior to the social order which we know as 'modern civilization' . . . . The most conspicuous special character of Indian culture, and its greatest significance for the modern world, is the evidence of a constant effort to understand the meaning and ultimate purpose of life, and a purposive

124

organization of society in harmony with that order, and with a view to the attainment of that purpose."[3]

I Caste: Its Metaphysical Basis

The institution of caste is typical of the Hindu social order. It has been the subject of bitter criticism in all ages, and particularly in modern times. It has also, however, been given credit for the amazing continuity of the Indian village community. Coomaraswamy's exposition of the traditional social philosophy is heavily dependent on his deeper examination of the caste system. His contention is that caste, in spite of the aberrations and injustices that have often derived sanction from it, is basically a sound solution to the problems involved in social relationships. Moreover, it is a *durable* solution, because it is grounded in the principles of the perennial philosophy on its metaphysical as well as its ethical side.

In order to understand the metaphysical basis of the traditional community, particularly as seen in the Indian social order, it would be helpful to recapitulate briefly the basic concepts which we have already noticed in our discussion of the perennial philosophy. In the first place, there is the idea of two perspectives: the transcendental and the empirical. Being in its essential nature is Absolute, Unconditioned, beyond the categories of time and space, beyond the operation of the causal law, and indescribable in terms of our limited, finite linguistic and ideational equipment. But Being also has an aspect of manifestation. Considered in this aspect, the world of time and space, of causal sequence, of valuational distinctions, has an indubitable relevance. So long as we function at the practical level, the universe must be viewed from the empirical perspective and our life in the universe must be taken seriously. Social organization is an important aspect of this life and should not be belittled on the ground that the world of becoming is only relatively real. Coomaraswamy repeatedly points out that in India the most absolute form of idealism at the metaphysical level has been combined with meticulous attention to the minutest details of man's life as a member of the community.

Second, and as a corollary to the above, the perennial philosophy refuses to see any contradiction between monism and pluralism, unity and diversity. The many are real from the empirical perspective, though the One alone is real from the metaphysical standpoint. The world of multiplicity and change is an appearance of the

Absolute, but it is a *real* appearance. The social institutions which
man has evolved are a part of this world of plurality and change.
They are grounded on the assumption that individuals have a real
stake in the manner in which their lives are related to the life of the
community and, beyond the community, to the life of the world,
including nature. Coomaraswamy points out that the great significance attached to the fourfold division of society in India is the
clearest refutation of the alleged world-denying and life-denying
attitude of Indian thought. Just as on the cosmic scale multiplicity
must be accepted in spite of the assumption of ultimate unity, so
also from the standpoint of man's social life diversity of temperament, aptitude, character, and vocation must be accepted in spite
of the fact that all men share a common origin — the Supreme
Spirit — and a common destiny, which is Liberation from the limits
and bonds of finitude. In the Indian social scheme this diversity,
based on man's multi-layered nature, has found expression without
disturbing the fundamental oneness of human endeavor.

Third, there is the idea of a universal, rhythmic flow of life in the
cosmos which all traditional philosophies share but which has
received particular emphasis in India. In the Vedas, this all-
pervading force is suggested by the concept of *rita,* the power which
ensures the reign of harmony and order everywhere in the manifested world. So important is *rita* that Varuna, the greatest of the
gods, is described as the Upholder of *Rita.* The working of *rita* is
seen in the cycle of the seasons, the growth of all sentient beings,
the movements of the planets, and all other natural phenomena. It
has its counterpart in the social life of man. To accept the orderli-
ness and the rhythmic character of the cosmos involves a commitment that we should participate in this *elan vital* and order our
affairs in such a way that the total harmony is not interrupted.
Coomaraswamy believes that the Hindu social scheme is founded
on this basic conviction. The idea that each individual should joyfully perform his allotted vocation, in accordance with his own
proper place in the life of the community, is derived logically and
naturally from the assumption that the entire phenomenal world is
sustained by a single rhythmic principle which is expressed in different ways in the various aspects of life in nature and in the human
community.

Finally, the connection between the metaphysical and the social
aspect of the perennial philosophy is to be seen in the profound
symbolism of the Sacrifice. The Absolute sacrifices its Oneness,

and the many are born. The maintenance of the world-process itself is to be understood as an "incessant process of Sacrifice" in which the Unconditioned joyfully suspends its essential nature and allows itself to be revealed in the world of causation, relationship, and conditioning. "This Sacrifice, performed *in divinis* by the All-Worker (Vishvakarma), as imitated here demands the cooperation of all the arts (vishva karmani).... The politics of the heavenly, social, and individual communities are governed by one and the same law."[4] The performance of the sacrificial ritual enjoyed by scripture — for instance, the offering of food to the Deity — is only a symbolic gesture expressing the meaning of the primeval Sacrifice.

Relating India's caste system to this concept, Coomaraswamy says, "In man, when the sacramental life is complete, there is a hierarchy of sacerdotal, royal, and administrative powers, and a fourth class consisting of the physical organs of sense and action that handle the raw material or 'food' to be prepared for all. And it is clear that if the organism is to flourish, which is impossible if divided against itself, the sacerdotal, royal, and administrative powers, in their order of rank, must be the 'masters' and the workers in raw materials their 'servants'.... The castes are literally 'born of the Sacrifice.' In the sacramental order there is a need and a place for all men's work. And there is no more significant consequence of the principle 'Work is Sacrifice' than the fact that, under these conditions, and remote as this may be from our secular way of thinking, every function, from that of the king and the priest down to that of the potter or the scavenger, is literally a priesthood, and every operation is a rite."[5]

II   *Caste: Its Ethical Basis*

In the perennial philosophy, as expounded by Ananda Coomaraswamy, ethics can be viewed from two different standpoints. From the transcendental or metaphysical standpoint, ethics is but a stepping-stone. Its value is relative. Its role is purely instrumental and in the state of liberation (*Mukti* or *Nirvana*) ethical judgments and distinctions must necessarily be left behind. But from the empirical standpoint, moral issues are supremely important. To ignore them would constitute a serious interruption of the principle of Law and Rhythm operating in the universe. Moral discrimination is part of man's natural endowment. Sooner or later, all of us must pass on from the Way of Desire to the Way of Righteousness, from *kama* and *artha* to *dharma.* The word *dharma* in Sanskrit means not only "duty" but also "essential nature." The transition from egoism to altruism is a normal phase in man's development. Not to make such a transition is an aberration.

In traditional societies there is no such thing as a purely individual ethical code. Man is a member of the community, the *polis.* In India, as in Greece, it was assumed that morality, like art, is something which men evolve and sustain in the process of living together in a community. Dharma is derived from, sanctioned by, and verified through man's social life. But since men differ from each other in intellect, ability, and emotional tone, *dharma* must reflect the differentiation as well as the oneness of man's life. It has a universal as well as a particular aspect. Man's ethical evaluations are determined by his sense of what is good and right without qualification, as well as by what is good and right *for him* as a member of a particular group and as the practitioner of a particular vocation. In other words there is a universal dharma which is binding on all, and also a *svadharma* — one's own special set of duties — determined by one's place in the social scheme.

Coomaraswamy sees in this concept of *svadharma* the ethical ground of the fourfold division of society accepted by Hinduism and popularly referred to as the caste system. The traditional name for this division is *varnashrama dharma.* Sometimes the word *vyavastha* ("system" or "arrangement") is also used. But in most cases the emphasis is on the individual's special obligation; and the fulfillment of this obligation is referred to as *dharma,* which clearly indicates the essentially ethical basis of the entire system. Contrasting the Hindu social order with modern industrial society, Coomaraswamy says, "The caste system differs from the industrial division of labor, with its fractioning of human faculties, in that it presupposes differences in *kinds* of responsibility but not in *degrees* of responsibility." And he adds that the modern sociologist paints the caste system in such dark colors "because an organization of functions such as this, with its mutual loyalties and duties, is absolutely incompatible with competitive industrialism." The sociologist fails to grasp the deeper meaning of caste because his "thinking is determined more by his actual environment than it is a deduction from first principles."[6]

Three points emerge from the above: first, that the traditional social order is backed by a clearly perceived philosophical world outlook (i.e., it is deduced from first principles); second, that it gives priority to obligation rather than to individual rights; and third, that it gives full recognition to diversity and emphasizes differences rather than equality. These characteristics are to be seen in the Platonic no less than in the Indian social ideal. Corresponding to the Brahmana, the Kshatriya, and the Vaishya in the Hindu social order, there are the three classes into which Plato divides society: the philosopher-ruler, the warrior, and the artisan. Plato assigns a *svadharma* — a special duty or virtue — to each class: wisdom (or reason), courage, and obedience. Justice is defined as the harmonious functioning of the three classes, each practicing the virtue appropriate to it. But the correspondence is only partial. Plato combines administrative and intellectual (rational) powers in a single class: "philosophers must be kings and kings must be philosophers." In the Indian social order, on the contrary, the sacerdotal (or spiritual as including intellectual) function is specially assigned to the Brahmanas, while the practical function — administration as well as defense, or the arts of war and peace — belongs to the Kshatriyas. In fact the Indian tradition disapproves of the "wise man" meddling in political affairs: he should stay away from the court but should be available for consultation. Another important difference between the Platonic and the Indian scheme is that the fourth class, consisting of those performing manual labor, does not find a place in Plato's scheme. His classification is limited to the Greeks. The barbarians and the slaves are excluded.

Coomaraswamy emphasizes that the caste system in India does not have a racial basis. In the early phases of Aryan settlement in India, ethnic differences were taken into account. The word *varna* indicates color or complexion. But in the centuries that followed races intermingled, and only vocational differences remained. These vocations were — and still largely are — hereditary. The theory of rebirth has always been accepted in India. The Hindu sociologists "assumed that by a natural law the individual ego is always, or nearly always, reborn into its own befitting environment." Coomaraswamy does not assert that this view was "proved" by formal argument. But he adds: "If the Hindu thinkers were wrong on this point, then it remains for others to discover some better way of achieving the same ends. I do not say that this is impossible. But it can hardly be denied that the Brahmanical caste system is the nearest approach that has yet been made towards a society where there shall be no attempt to realize a competitive equality, but where all interests are regarded as identical."[7]

To understand the ideal on which the system is based, it is necessary to reconstruct imaginatively the manner in which the ancient social thinkers must have argued. According to Coomaraswamy: "The Brahmana sociologists were firmly convinced that in an ideal society, i.e. a society designed deliberately by man for the fulfillment of his own purpose (*purushartha*), not only must opportunity be allowed to every one for such experience as his spiritual status requires, but also that the best and wisest must rule. It seemed to them impossible that an ideal society should have any other than an aristocratic basis, the aristocracy being at once intellectual and spiritual. . . . 'If,' thought they, 'we can determine natural classes, then let us assign to each its appropriate duties (*svadharma,* own norm) and appropriate honor; this will at once facilitate a convenient division of necessary labor, ensure the handing down of hereditary skill in pupillary succession, avoid all possibility of social ambition, and allow to every individual the experience and activity which he needs and owes.' "[8]

The classes recognized in the Hindu caste system "constitute the natural hierarchy of human society." Coomaraswamy asserts that, although in practice caste has been the source of discrimination and even oppression, the system in itself is neither unjust nor tyrannical. The lot of the *Shudra* has often been described as miserable. But the system has some important safeguards which critics tend to ignore, declares Coomaraswamy. "The nature of the difference between a Brahman and a Shudra is indicated in the view that a Shudra can do no wrong, a view that must make an immense demand upon the patience of the higher castes, and is the absolute converse of the Western doctrine that the king can do no wrong." Coomaraswamy also points out that in the orthodox scheme the lowest caste is free from certain restrictions imposed upon the higher castes: for instance in such matters as diet, dress, widow remarriage. And it is recommended that in sentencing a wrong-doer or a criminal, Coomaraswamy adds, "the punishment of the Vaishya should be twice as heavy as that of the Shurdra; that of the Kshatriya twice as heavy again; and that of the Brahman twice or even four times as heavy again in respect of the same offense, for responsibility rises with intelligence and status."[9]

Coomaraswamy also rejects the charge that in the caste system the voice of the common man is not heard. "Given the natural classes," he asserts, "one of the good elements of what is now regarded as democracy was provided by making the castes self-governing. Thus it was secured that a man should be tried by his peers (whereas under Industrial Democracy an artist may be tried by a jury of tradesmen, or a poacher by a bench of squires). Within the caste there existed equality of opportunity for all, and the caste as a body had collective privileges and responsibilities. Society thus organized has much the appearance of what would now be called Guild Socialism."[10]

III   *Spiritual Basis of the State*

Once the metaphysical and ethical roots of the traditional social philosophy are grasped, it does not make much difference how the practical issues of political and economic structure are dealt with. Coomaraswamy says, "Political and economic questions, though they cannot be ignored, are the most external and the least part of our problem. It is not through them that understanding can be reached. On the contrary, it is through understanding that political and economic problems can be solved."[11] By "understanding" Coomaraswamy means a perception of the deeper purpose of the state, leading to an agreement on fundamentals and flexibility on questions of detail.

Coomaraswamy's writings do not yield any detailed statement of his political views because he considers political and economic issues "external," and his own concern is with the inner relationship of man's social life with a universally valid conception of the real and the good. Nevertheless, three points emerge quite clearly from his political attitudes. In the first place, Coomaraswamy insists on the spiritual foundation of the state and rejects the view that politics are governed inherently by considerations of power, profit, or expediency rather than by ideals. He believes that the ancient Hindu ideal of kingship was based on a firm recognition of the spiritual foundation of the state. "There is a fundamental difference," he says, "between the Brahman and the modern view of politics. The modern politician considers that idealism in politics is unpractical. . . . The Western sociologist is apt to say: 'The teachings of religion and philosophy may or may not be true, but in any case they have no significance for the practical reformer." The Brahmans, on the contrary, considered all activity not directed in accordance with a consistent theory of the meaning and purpose of life to be supremely unpractical.''[12]

Although he uses the term *Brahman view,* Coomaraswamy's reference is to the ancient Indian tradition as a whole, and not merely to the Hindu attitude. The ideal of kingship expressed in the inspiring life of Shri Rama has always struck a responsive chord in the mind and heart of the average Indian. The *Rāmāyana* is, indeed, the most representative example of the Indian vision of a perfect state. *Rama Rajya* (Rule of Rama) is a term which has become synonymous with good and just government. Nevertheless, it was the Buddhist emperor, Ashoka, who for the first time in history abjured violence as an instrument of authority and organized a vast empire based entirely on the power of love. Coomaraswamy points out that Ashoka's long reign of nearly forty years was not interrupted by any rebellion, in spite of the fact that military officers were replaced by *dharmamahāmātras* (Officers of Righteousness) whose duty was to spread the Buddha's message of *metteya* (Friendliness). While his internal administration was based on the concept of universal tolerance, Ashoka's foreign policy was guided by the maxim that a nation does not acquire glory through territorial conquests but by conquest through love. Coomaraswamy quotes passages from Ashoka's edicts as illustrating the Indian ideal of statesmanship: "His Sacred Majesty desires that all animate beings should have security, peace of mind, and joyousness.... My sons and grandsons, who may be, should not regard it as a duty to make a new conquest.... They should take pleasure in patience and gentleness, and regard as the only true conquest that which is won by piety. That avails both for this world and the next."[13]

The second point which must be mentioned in connection with Coomaraswamy's political comments is that he questions the assumption that modern democracy is necessarily the best form of government: "If it is decided that every man's voice is to count equally in the councils of the nation, it follows naturally that the voice of those who think must be drowned by that of those who do not think and have no leisure. This position leaves all classes alike at the mercy of unscrupulous individual exploitation, for all political effort lacking a philosophical basis becomes opportunist."[14] As for freedom, there can be a tyranny of the majority as galling as the tyranny of a minority or an individual. "Consider a community of five," says Coomaraswamy. "It is impossible to deny that the rule of three, so far as it affects the other two, is as much an arbitrary constraint as the rule of one affecting the other four. It is very liable to be less intelligent."[15] If one looks at the canvas of history over the centuries, happiness and contentment have often marked periods of benevolent despotism, while tension and conflict have often characterized those ages when human affairs have been decided by the sheer weight of numbers. What counts is the real autonomy of the individual, irrespective of whether this autonomy is secured through the wisdom and imagination of a single outstanding individual or through deliberations culminating in the majority vote.

Going a little deeper into the question of individual autonomy, Coomaraswamy reverts to the idea that enduring solutions to social problems are possible only on the basis of *dharma*. Where the approach is materialistic and competitive, the inner freedom of the individual is sacrificed at the altar of political power. But when a man "sees the Self in all things and all things in the Self,"[16] there is no conflict between personal freedom and communal responsibility. Politics, Coomaraswamy asserts, can be viewed either in the spirit of ego-assertion or in the spirit of renunciation. Paradoxical as it may sound, he declares, they govern best who have repudiated the will to govern: "Only a renunciation of the will to govern can create a stable equilibrium. . . . Only he is an individualist in truth who does not have the will to govern any one but himself."[17] Referring to Nietzsche's "Will to Power," Coomaraswamy says, "The 'will to govern' must not be confused with the 'will to power.' The will to govern is the will to govern others. The will to power is the will to govern oneself."[18] Thus from the side of politics we are led back to the central concept of Self-conquest on which *dharma* is founded.

Before this section on Coomaraswamy's political views is concluded, a brief reference should be made to his attitude towards nationalism. He was an ardent nationalist in the sense that he loved the national culture of India (of which he regarded Shri Lankā to be an integral part), worked for its preservation and appreciation, and criticized the damage done to it by colonial exploitation and an alien system of education. But he saw the dangers of a political philosophy based on extreme forms of nationalism. Long before the emergence of chauvinistic nationalist movements in Europe, Asia, and Africa, Coomaraswamy warned that patriotism, unless it is illumined by an idealistic ethos, might become a dangerous weapon in the hands of unscrupulous politicians. "The pure politi-

cian," he pointed out, "is often no nationalist at all, in the idealistic sense. The Kingdom of Heaven is within us; so also is the freedom of nations."[19] The mere absence of the foreigner does not
make a country independent, and the nationalist whose aim is only
to replace one bureaucracy by another has a very narrow conception of his country's destiny. "The Pole adhering to his language
and traditions, preserving his character and individuality, is more
free despite his fetters than Indians would be tomorrow if every
foreigner left their shores."[20]

Nationalism defined in terms of purely political or economic
ends, and expressed mainly through political and economic struggle, is bound to become a divisive force in world affairs, Coomaraswamy believed. But if a nation's pride in its own inheritance and
its dreams of its own future are based on a recognition of the
fundamental principle of unity in diversity, nationalism can
become a creative force bringing together men of sincerity, vision,
and good will from the ends of the earth. For after all, Coomaraswamy asks, "How can there be any divergence of idealism from
idealism?" Speaking specifically of India, he says, "It is life, and
not merely Indian life, that claims our loyalty.... The chosen
people of the future cannot be any nation or race, but an aristocracy of the earth combining the virility of European youth with the
serenity of Asiatic age.... The flowering of humanity is more to us
than the victory of any party. The only condition of a renewal of
life in India should be a spiritual, and not merely an economic or
political, awakening."[21]

IV   *The Status of Women*

At no other feature of traditional societies has the accusing
finger of the modern critic been pointed more persistently and
vigorously than at the status of women. And the accusation is all
the sharper when the lot of the oriental woman is referred to. Western writers do not seem to tire of repeating that even in medieval
Europe the condition of women, in spite of all the handicaps and
iniquities suffered by them, was infinitely superior to that of Indian
women in the modern age. In India, the woman is man's chattel.
She has no will or personality of her own; and if she had it, she
would have no opportunity of expressing it. She is denied education, has no authority in the home or outside, has no right to the
joys of comradeship or love, and is completely dependent upon

men for the bare necessities of life. Such is the picture of Indian
womanhood that most modern writers have drawn. On this point
Indians themselves are usually defensive in modern times.

Coomaraswamy examines all these questions with his usual thor-
oughness and tries to view them in the perspective of the total
Indian tradition. He does not deny that, in its present state of
decline, Indian society does not give its women the position of
honor and responsibility they once occupied. But he points out that
modern Western concepts of happiness and freedom cannot provide the criteria for judging the status or condition of Indian
women. These criteria must be derived from values and ideals that
have stood the test of centuries and have been accepted in all ages
of Indian history. And the ideals themselves are based on metaphysical and ethical assumptions which must be taken into account.

According to the Indian view, the male and the female represent
two aspects of reality itself in its manifest state. In the famous
Shiva image at Elephanta the Lord of the Universe is depicted as
Ardhanārishvara (God who is Half Woman). The modelling of the
face, the expression of the eyes, the head-gear, the jewelry and the
anatomical features — all these are masculine on one side of the
image, feminine on the other. Even in other images of Shiva — for
instance in Shiva as Nataraja (Lord of Dancers), — the symbolism
is suggested by two different types of earrings, one of them being
appropriate to Uma. It is significant that in religious ritual every
important god is worshipped along with his spouse: Shiva and Par-
vati, Rama and Sita, Krishna and Radha, Brahma and Sarasvati,
Vishnu and Lakshmi. In popular usage the goddess is usually mentioned before the god. Thus it is more natural to say Sita-Rama and
Radha-Krishna than to say Rama-Sita or Krishna-Radha. In the
Hindu pantheon, the feminine form is thus raised to the status of
divinity almost on equal terms with the masculine. The Divine is
worshipped as goddesses visualized as terrible, like Kali, or gentle
and compassionate, like Uma and Lakshmi, or beautiful, like
Sarasvati. Buddhism, too, in course of time evolved its own female
deities, among whom Tara is the most striking, since she combines
beauty with power.[22]

The world process demands the combination of consciousness
and energy. Without energy, consciousness would be passive; without consciousness, energy would be blind, purposeless, devoid of
pattern or design. Symbolically, the male form embodies consciousness, the female form represents energy. "As pure male, the

Great God is inert, and his 'power' is always feminine, and it is she who leads the hosts of heaven against the demons," declares Coomaraswamy.[23] The union of Shiva and Shakti, of consciousness and power, is conveyed through the metaphor of conjugal love. The close embrace of male and female forms in some of the great masterpieces of Indian sculpture conveys this profound truth of the twofold nature of the Real. What is nothing but erotica to many Western art historians is actually a depiction in stone of the "One which is also two, without ceasing to be One." The allegory is carried forward in miniature painting, in the glorious Vaishnava love lyrics about Radha and Krishna, and even in music, where *rāgas* have their corresponding spouses (rāginis).

Woman is glorified not only as the consort of the Divine but also as Mother. She is the principle of fruitfulness, of fertility, of the perpetuation of life. Many are the forms in which the Divine Mother has received the adoration of devotees. And her earthly counterparts, the mothers in Indian families, have always been treated with utmost love and reverence. Coomaraswamy quotes these words from Manu: "A master exceedeth ten tutors in claim to honor; the father a hundred masters; but the mother a thousand fathers in the right to reverence and in the function of teacher."[24] Travelers who came to India in ancient times — Greeks as well as Chinese — testify to the exceptional status of the mother in Indian homes. "According to the Tantrik scriptures, devoted to the cult of the Mother of the World, women — who partake of her nature more essentially than other living beings, are especially honored; here the woman may be a spiritual teacher (*guru*), and the initiation of a son by a mother is more fruitful than any other," writes Coomaraswamy.[25]

The principle of vitality in nature is regarded as feminine. This principle is represented in many beautiful ways by the figures of the *Yakshī* or *Vrikshakā* (dryad, tree goddess) or *Vana-devatā* (forest deity) which adorn so many Hindu and Buddhist monuments. The Yakshi leans against a tree or touches the tree with one of her feet. At her touch, the tree bursts into blossom. One of her hands is placed on her waist, suggesting a dance posture. With the other hand, raised above her head, she clasps a flower-laden branch. She pulsates with the breath of life which sustains nature. She is vigorous, yet nimble; dynamic, yet utterly relaxed. Her eyes are half closed, indicating inward joy and tranquility. With all the grace of an accomplished dancer she personifies the gently surging life-sap within the tree. Such is the conception of Woman, in which beauty and sacredness are fused together — a conception which exalts Woman as the animating power behind all that lives, the preserver of the rhythm which flows through all beings and establishes the harmony in nature.[26]

Let us now turn from the philosophical to the ethical basis of the Indian attitude to women. The idea of Dharma is based on a recognition of real differences in all spheres of human life. Human beings are multi-layered. There are many sides to man's nature and, as we have seen earlier, this manysidedness is accepted in Hindu social organization as well as in the various paths suggested for the attainment of liberation. Since the qualities of men and women differ, their roles must also be correspondingly different. Coomaraswamy points out that this fact has been recognized in all non-industrial societies. He quotes from Novalis: "The sexes are differently entertained. Man demands the sensational in intellectual form, woman the intellectual in sensational form. What is secondary to the man is paramount to the woman. Do they not resemble the Infinite, since it is impossible to square them, and they can only be approached through approximation?"[27] The same line of thinking is seen in the Indian view which is "not that man and woman should approach an identity of temperament and function, but that for the greatest abundance in life there is requisite the greatest possible sexual differentiation."[28]

Woman can realize the best within herself by performing the role that is distinctively hers — the role that is natural to her because it is determined by her biological and psychological differentiation from man. Coomaraswamy writes: "The governing concept of Hindu ethics is vocation (*dharma*); the highest merit consists in fulfillment of one's own duty, in other words, in dedication to one's own calling. . . . Indian society was highly organized; and where it was considered wrong even for a man to fulfill the duties of another man rather than his own, how much more must a confusion of function as between man and woman have seemed wrong, where differentiation is so much more evident."[29] The natural roles of women are those of the wife and the mother. Under special circumstances women in India have attained great distinction in social or religious service, in the arts, even in politics. But writes Coomaraswamy, "Hindu sociologists have always regarded these specializations as more or less incompatible with wifehood and motherhood; life is not long enough for the achievement of many different things."[30] In the very performance of these roles, he continues, they contribute to the preservation of *dharma*. "In the words of Manu: 'To be mothers were women created, and to be fathers men'; and he adds significantly: 'therefore are religious sacraments ordained in the Veda by the husband together with the wife." The wife is often referred to as *sahadharmacharini*, that is "she who walks with her husband on the path of dharma."

Such, then, is the philosophical and ethical basis of the Indian concept of womanhood. But when one turns from ideals to facts, it may be questioned whether the status of women in India has actually been as low as Western critics have asserted. The housewife has real authority in the Indian home, and all decisions concerning household management are usually left to her judgment.[31] Even Manu, whose writings are often quoted in support of the alleged ill-treatment of women, declares that the level of a society is best judged in proportion to the honor that is paid to women. Passages from the *Rāmāyana* are sometimes quoted to show the inferior status of women. But the *Rāmāyana* also contains other passages in which Sita emerges as Rama's comrade rather than as his subservient wife. Women have played a much more significant part in the cultural, and even political, history of India than in European history. In the *Upanishads* we read about women philosophers like Gārgī and Maitreyī with whom great sages like Yājnavalkya discuss abstruse metaphysical questions. Some of the greatest names in Indian poetry are those of women: Avvai in the south and Mirabai in the north, to mention only two. In his *Rājatarangini,* Kalhana describes the pivotal role which some remarkable queens filled in the history of Kashmir.[32] In the reign of Jahangir, when the Mughal Empire was at the height of its prosperity, it was the Empress, Nur Jahan, who really governed India. And she proved a wise, efficient, benevolent, and cultured sovereign. The careers of Chand Bibi, Ahalya Bai, and Lakshmi Bai (Rani of Jhansi) bear ample testimony to the fact India could produce heroic and amazonian no less than tender types of women.

The disparagement of oriental women is usually based on their alleged lack of freedom. But is freedom to be understood only as the right of self-expression? Moreover, what is the "self" for which we are demanding this right of expression? "Hinduism," says Coomaraswamy, "justifies no cult of ego-expression, but aims consistently at spiritual freedom. Those who are conscious of a sufficient inner life become the more indifferent to outward expression of their own or any changing personality."[33] In the Indian view, expression of the Self is to be judged in terms of a larger harmony, a more enduring well-being, rather than in terms of the ability to get what one wants and do what one pleases. In Coomaraswamy's words, "The ultimate purposes of Hindu social discipline are that men should unify their individuality with a wider and deeper than individual life, should fulfill appointed tasks regardless of failure or success, distinguish the timeless from its shifting forms, and escape the all-too-narrow prison of the 'I and mine.' " Freedom is an inner condition. It is not the absence of restraint so much as the absence of inner tensions. If freedom is seen as tranquility or the release from fear, anxiety, agitation, and envy, the oriental women, Coomaraswamy asserts, are far more free than their European sisters.[34]

Marriage based on free choice is sometimes mentioned as the proof of freedom for women. Coomaraswamy writes: "Current Western theory seeks to establish marriage on the basis of romantic love; marriage thus depends on the accident of 'falling in love.' Those who are 'crossed in love' or are not in love are not required to marry. This individualistic position is, however, only logically defensible if at the same time it is recognized that to fall out of love must end the marriage."[35] This position is inescapable so long as the West places rights above duties and equates release from responsibility with independence. Coomaraswamy continues: "For Hindu sociologists marriage is a social and ethical relationship, and the begetting of children is the payment of a debt. Romantic love is a brief experience of timeless freedom, essentially religious and ecstatic, in itself as purely anti-social as every glimpse of Union is a denial of the Relative."[36] In India, Coomaraswamy points out, it is assumed that "happiness will arise from the fulfillment of vocation, far more than when immediate satisfaction is made the primary end." And he adds, "I use the term 'vocation' advisedly; for the oriental marriage ... is the fulfillment of a traditional design, and does not depend upon the accidents of sensibility. To be such a man as Rama, such a wife as Sita, rather than to 'express oneself,' is the aim."[37] In this light one can appreciate the injunction that the husband should be regarded as a god, irrespective of his merit or demerit. The words should not be taken literally. The idea they convey is that "it would be beneath a woman's dignity to deviate from her norm merely because of the failure of a man. It is for her own sake and for the sake of the community, rather than for his alone, that life must be attuned to the eternal unity of Purusha and Prakriti."

Referring to Western criticism of the oriental criterion of "adjustment" as a negation of freedom, Coomaraswamy says, "We can only reply that we do not identify freedom with self-assertion, and that the oriental woman is what she is, only because our social and religious culture has permitted her to be and to remain essentially feminine." She has not been judged in terms of knowledge or efficiency, not even in terms of obedience or self-effacement — though it may appear so on the surface — but in terms of those qualities which are distinctively hers. "The one thing that men have demanded of her is Life" — life which woman makes sweeter by her tenderness and brighter by her radiance. For Coomaraswamy, "Radha's shining made the ground she stood on bright as gold.... It is this radiance in women, more than any other quality, that urges men to every sort of heroism, be it martial or poetic."[38]

As for the much-vaunted progress of Western women, Coomaraswamy points out that the competitive spirit of modern industrial societies, which are in their very nature based on exploitation, robs woman of much that is truly precious in human life. He adds, "Let us not deceive ourselves that because the Western marriage is nominally founded upon free choice, it therefore secures a permanent unity of spiritual or physical passion." Where there is so much emphasis on material comforts and legal (rather than moral) rights, marriage is bound to be deficient in that element of contentment and serenity without which there can be no lasting union between individuals. Thousands of women in Western societies remain single. Hundreds of thousands of marriages end in separation or divorce, leaving a trail of frustration and bitterness, and causing incalculable harm to the offspring. And yet Western society refuses to reexamine its premises regarding the nature of freedom and happiness. The ironical aspect of the situation is that women themselves do not realize the contradiction upon which their own movement for emancipation is founded — the contradiction inherent in the acceptance of *male values* while struggling against male domination. They fail to see that the real need is to gain "the right to be themselves rather than the right to become more like men." While the oriental woman gives her all to the home and the community, and retains the right to be feminine, the Western woman asserts her right of equality with men at the cost of her femininity.[39]

Far from indicating self-confidence or human dignity, the struggle for equality often betrays self-distrust on the part of women. "The so-called feminist is as much enslaved by masculine ideals," Coomaraswamy points out, "as the so-called Indian nationalist is enslaved by European ideals." The modern woman "values industry more than leisure"; her ambition is "to externalize her life and achieve success in men's professions." And all the while, "in proportion to her loss of genuine feminine idealism," she loses her true strength, the source of her real power, declares Coomaraswamy. "The argument that women can do what men can do — like the argument that Indians can be prepared to govern themselves by a course of studies in democracy — implies a profound distrust. The claim of equality with men, or with Englishmen — what an honor! That men, or Englishmen, as the case may be, should grant the claim — what a condescension!"[40]

I will conclude this account of Coomaraswamy's views on the role of women in society by pointing to two possible misconceptions. In the first place, some of his remarks might leave the impression that he is suggesting a reversion to ancient or medieval social conditions. Anticipating this objection, he says, "To avoid misunderstanding, let me say . . . that in depicting the life of Hindu women as fulfilling a great ideal, I do not indicate the Hindu social formula as a thing to be repeated or imitated. This would be a view as futile as the Gothic revival in architecture. The reproduction of period furniture does not belong to life. A perfection that has been can never be a perfection for us."[41] Secondly, Coomaraswamy does *not* look upon the Indian concept of womanhood as something unique, something for which the wise men of ancient India should be given special credit. Until the industrial revolution, and the consequent overturning of the values derived from the *Philosophia Perennis,* the West also accepted that concept. Coomaraswamy refers to many Western counterparts of the ideal women glorified in Indian myth, legend, and history: Helen, of whom it was said that "strangely like she was to some immortal spirit"; Deirdre, who refused every offer of protection and care from Conchubar; Emer, who refused to live after the death of Cuchullain (like an Indian *sati*); Brynhild, who was no less devoted to Sigurd than Savitri was to Satyavān or Damayantī to Nala.[42]

"The oriental woman," Coomaraswamy asserts, "is perhaps not oriental at all, but simply woman."[43] He does not claim that the Indian woman is superior to women of other lands in her innermost nature: "She is perhaps an older, purer and more specialized type, but certainly an universal type, and it is precisely here that the industrial woman departs from type. Nobility in women does not depend upon race, but upon ideals; it is the outcome of a certain view of life." All that he maintains is that in the East, and especially in India, women have preserved some of the aspects of a harmonious life-style which the West has interrupted in the modern age; and that women in India are, on the whole, better adjusted, inwardly more free, and happier than Western women. In support of this assertion he offers a very simple criterion: "One has only to return to London from any oriental country and contrast the facial expression of most women there with the facial expression of most women in the East to realize that the latter are the happier."[44]

V   *Education: Modern and Traditional*

Like Plato, whom he admired so much, Coomaraswamy had a firm faith in the "teachability of mankind." It was this faith that sustained his optimism in spite of the mechanization and dehumanization of life in modern industrial society. He attributed many of the conflicts and tensions of our age to the "neglect of education in first principles." And the first step in reconciliation, he asserted, was the "reeducation of the Western literati."[45] The term *education* here does not refer to formal acquisition of knowledge but to a process of inward refinement, leading to an understanding of the meaning, purpose, and possibilities of human life, and a creative reconstruction of society in the light of that understanding.

While many of Coomaraswamy's comments on the subject of education are applicable to the modern world as a whole, his special concern was with problems of education in Asian countries, especially India (including Shri Lankā). In this, he was in line with the great leaders of modern India — Gandhi, Tagore, Radhakrishnan, Shri Aurobindo — who saw in education the key to the regeneration of their country's life and culture. It would therefore be appropriate to begin our study of Coomaraswamy's educational views by referring to his assessment of the Western and the traditional types of education as seen in the Indian situation.

"The aim of education," Coomaraswamy reminds us "should be not so much the levelling up of faculties and the production of uniform types as the intensive cultivation of the faculties we already have.''[46] By this criterion, the system of education introduced by the British in India contradicted the basic aim which a good teacher must adopt. English education in India did nothing to discover, much less to encourage, the natural talents of the pupils. Coomaraswamy quotes Ruskin's remark that education means "finding out what people have tried to do, and helping them to do it better." And he adds, "There has been no 'finding out' in India, but only a complete inversion of values."[47] The most urgent need, therefore, was to reexamine the very foundation on which the structure of education in India was being built. National leaders harp on "Indianization" of political institutions and financial enterprises, declares Coomaraswamy. "But much more important than political or economic reform is the demand for complete control of Indian education in all its branches."[48]

The majority of British educators in India, and their Indian imitators and admirers, proceeded on the basis of Macaulay's assumption that the aim of modern education in India should be to create a class of people "Indian in blood and race but British in taste and character."[49] But some discerning Westerners have not failed to realize the harm done to Asian countries by the imposition of an alien and unnatural system of education. Coomaraswamy quotes Lord Birdwood's opinion, expressed as far back as 1880: "Our education has destroyed their love of their own literature . . . and their delight in their own arts."[50] As the result of foreign education the intellectuals of India and Shri Lankā, says Coomaraswamy, have permitted "the decay of those elements in our culture which constitute its greatness" and have "acquired in exchange a superficial veneer of Western civilization."[51] In this education "physical science is divorced from philosophy," which is in utter violation of India's ancient tradition, and the learner's mind is bound "in a superstition of facts more difficult to escape from than any superstition of the fancy in the past."[52]

Education which is not related to the accumulated experience and the cherished ideals of a country can be worse than useless. It can be confusing, frustrating, and demoralizing. Coomaraswamy again quotes the views of Ruskin: "Do not disturb their reverence for the past. Do not think that your mission is to dispel their ignorance. . . Teach them only gentleness and truth. Cherish above all things local associations and hereditary skills."[53] The pedagogical methods and attitudes of Western educators in India and Shri Lankā were the very reverse of Ruskin's wise advice. And the most

tragic aspect of the situation was that upperclass Indians themselves, instead of expressing their opposition, welcomed the artificial and snobbish products of this kind of education. They felt flat-
tered and thought that the summit of their ambition would be
attained if their children "picked up a little French" or "learnt a
few strokes on the violin" at finishing schools.[54] It did not matter
to them if the children did not learn even the rudiments of their
own mother-tongue and remained ignorant of the noble thoughts
and colorful life reflected in their own myths, legends, stories, epics
and ballads, their own music and dance.

Coomaraswamy's criticism was not directed against Western
education as a whole but only against those aspects of it which
reflected the materialistic, expediency-oriented and exclusively
intellectual values of modern industrial society. He was aware of
the new progressive movements in European education which
called for a humane and noncompetitive spirit in education. These
new movements attached great importance to each country's own
cultural inheritance in the planning of its educational system. But
educators in India ignored these trends. Coomaraswamy exhorted
them to visit Europe, America, and Japan and see the experiments
that were being made to reconstruct education in the light of
national traditions. "Let our education be more European in spirit
and less European in form," he suggested. "The spirit of modern
European education is national."[55]

In his assessment of traditional education in India, Coomaraswamy stresses its close connection with the metaphysical assumptions and the ethical ideals upon which Indian society is founded.
These assumptions and ideals are expressed concretely in the *Ramayana,* the *Mahabharata* and the Puranic legends, through stories of
heroes and gods. The Indian educators made full use of this vast
literature with which the child became familiar at a very early age.
According to Coomaraswamy, "The heroes themselves were made
ideal types of character, and the education of India has been
accomplished deliberately through hero-worship."[56] This deliberate education, based on precept and example, was constantly sup-
plemented by the unconscious assimilation of traditional values in
the very process of living. Where life is integrated, where education
is neither exclusively intellectual in its aims nor analytical in its
methods, and where human life is carried on in close communion
with the life of nature, learning begins long before the learner is
formally entrusted to the care of a teacher.

In traditional education, the importance of reading and writing is recognized but not exaggerated. Coomaraswamy quotes from the *Garuda Purana:* "Reading, to a man devoid of wisdom, is like a mirror to the blind." Formal literacy is no guarantee of knowledge, nor is illiteracy synonymous with ignorance. Some of the greatest and wisest men in history were formally illiterate. Muhammad, the Prophet of Islam, could barely read or write; and yet some of his compositions are among the most poetic in the Arabic language. Akbar, one of the greatest monarchs in history, was illiterate. But that did not prevent him from discussing intelligently many abstruse questions of religion and philosophy with learned representatives of different faiths and schools. Even in the modern age we have the example of Shri Ramakrishna, who was hardly able to sign his name and yet showed deep knowledge of metaphysical and ethical doctrines.

What is true of individuals is also true of groups and communities. Illiterate peoples can be cultured and can be described as "educated" in the deeper meaning of the term. Conversely, societies with a high percentage of formally educated people may be crude, insensitive, or even barbarous. Coomaraswamy recalls Plato's warning against excessive dependence on writing. "The wise man, when in earnest," says Plato, "will not write in ink dead words that cannot teach the truth, but will sow the seeds of wisdom in souls that are able to receive them, and so pass them on for ever."[57] In India there has been, for four millenia, a living tradition of orally transmitted wisdom. This is an inexhaustible treasure-house upon which the educator of our age can continue to draw. Coomaraswamy's point is that, while recognizing the urgency of educational expansion, we should not harbor illusions about the magical powers of reading and writing. "Is it more important to read and write," he asks, "than to let master minds sway the hearts of men? Can the Board of Education do more than what Valmiki, Tulsidas, Kamban and Manikka Vachagar have already done indirectly?"[58]

Modern education is becoming increasingly impersonal. In India's traditional education, on the contrary, supreme importance was attached to personal communication between the teacher and the student. Coomaraswamy quotes Sister Nivedita's remark: "Men are of greater consequence than curricula." Where the personal touch is lacking, education inevitably tends to become utilitarian and mechanical. It no longer trains young minds in the most satisfying and important of all arts: the art of living. Coomaraswamy's message to Young India is, "Let us learn to live rather than to accumulate the means of living."[59]

In the following passage Coomaraswamy sums up the ancient Indian theory of education: "The Brahmans attached no value to uncoordinated knowledge or to unearned opinions, but rather regarded these as dangerous tools in the hands of unskilled craftsmen. The greatest stress is laid on the development of character. Proficiency in hereditary aptitudes is assured by pupillary succession within the caste. But it is in respect of what we generally understand by higher education that the Brahman method differs most from modern ideals; for it is not even contemplated as desirable that all knowledge should be made accessible to all. The key to education is to be found in personality. There should be no teacher for whom teaching is less than a vocation (none may 'sell the Vedas'), and no teacher should impart his knowledge to a pupil until he finds the pupil ready to receive it, and the proof of this is to be found in the asking of the right questions. 'As the man who digs with a spade obtains water, even so an obedient pupil obtains the knowledge which is in his teacher.' "[60]

CHAPTER 7

Epilogue

IN a tribute to Ananda Coomaraswamy, Rabindranath Tagore once said, "Whatever we may call him — an art critic or a historian or simply a scholar — we find something is left over, something in his work which is indefinable. Ananda Coomaraswamy exceeds all our definitions. All our definitions fall short of his achievement. He is always something else."

Our discussion of Coomaraswamy's work and thought confirms Tagore's judgment. No labels can be attached to his ideas, nor can they be affiliated to this or that school or theory. But if his thought defies classification it is not because Coomaraswamy is eclectic or ambiguous; it is rather because he views human life and culture in their entirety, refuses to approach them piecemeal, and sees in them the expression of certain universal principles. These universal principles constitute, in a very broad sense, what he describes as the perennial philosophy. His commitment is only to this "traditional wisdom" which provides general guidelines but is sufficiently flexible to enable its exponents to dispense with sectarian molds. So thorough is Coomaraswamy's grasp of fundamentals that he can be definite without being dogmatic and show extraordinary expertise in particular fields of scholarship without becoming a narrow specialist. He sees in the perennial philosophy, from Plato to Ramakrishna, the expression of an impulse which transcends differences of age and country. But his exposition is not a mere assertion of continuity. It is marked by originality of interpretation, perception of unseen relationships, and rediscovery of forgotten meanings. In this sense Coomaraswamy — to repeat Tagore's words — exceeds all our definitions and "is always something else."

In the introductory chapter I have drawn attention to some of the characteristic features of Coomaraswamy's work and his distinctive contributions. In the present chapter I will attempt an assessment of Coomaraswamy's place in modern Indian thought, particularly in relation to the ideas of the two most influential Indian thinkers of our age: Gandhi and Tagore. I will conclude this essay with a brief critical review of Coomaraswamy's work.

I   Coomaraswamy, Gandhi, and Tagore

There are certain attitudes which Coomaraswamy shares with all the leading thinkers of modern India. These may be listed, for the sake of convenience, as follows:

1. A conviction that the reconstruction of India's life can only be attempted on the basis of her own tradition and not through imitation of alien, especially Western, norms.

2. Acceptance of the value of *all* the elements in Indian culture — Hindu, Buddhist, Jaina, Islamic, and Christian — and a firm rejection of sectarian or partisan interpretations.

3. As a corollary to the above, a pluralistic approach to life, based on the typically Indian view that "many paths lead to the same goal."

4. Emphasis on the spiritual side of life and rejection of the materialistic world view, while recognizing the importance of man's worldly concerns.

5. Preference for the integral rather than the analytical approach to culture, and a strong belief that the philosophical, the religious, and the aesthetic impulses cannot be considered in isolation from each other.

While the leading thinkers of modern India seem to show a broad agreement on these points, there are differences of emphasis which account for the diversity of modern Indian thought. In order to understand Coomaraswamy's own emphases, it would be interesting as well as helpful to adopt the comparative method and see his ideas in juxtaposition with those of Rabindranath Tagore and Mahatma Gandhi. So dominant and charismatic were the personalities of Tagore and Gandhi, the two "makers of modern India," that their younger contemporaries inevitably felt the impact of both of them in one way or another. Jawaharlal Nehru found himself gravitating alternately towards each of them and once said, "My mind is with Tagore, but how can I help it if my heart is held captive by the Mahatma!" And examination of Coomaraswamy's views shows that he, too, was closer to Gandhi in some respects but felt greater affinity with Tagore on some other points.

Coomaraswamy's approach to the Indian tradition was primarily aesthetic rather than ethical or social. This in itself explains his closeness to Tagore. Both Coomaraswamy and Tagore responded more enthusiastically to the aesthetic than to any other side of life: the former as historian and critic, the latter as a creative artist. Another bond between them was their cosmopolitanism. They were both intensely aware of the limits and dangers of nationalism and were internationalists in the finest sense of the term. Mahatma Gandhi was so much immersed in the problems of India that he gave very little attention to developments in other parts of the world, either in social or in cultural affairs. On several occasions when he was asked to give his opinion on international issues, he is said to have remarked with characteristic humility, "What do I know of these things? You should go to Jawaharlal Nehru." For his philosophical principles Gandhi claimed universal validity. But after his return from South Africa he applied those principles wholly in the Indian context. Tagore travelled extensively throughout the world and was in close personal communication with leading artists, writers, and thinkers of many countries. Moreover, his wide reading of Western literature enabled him to appreciate the Western point of view in different fields of culture. Coomaraswamy was a bit of a recluse, but his grounding in non-Indian cultures — especially Chinese and European — was much more thorough and systematic than that of Tagore. And he had the advantage of direct access to primary sources through his attainments as a linguist. Both Tagore and Coomaraswamy became such fine spokesmen of the Indian tradition because they were equipped to comprehend that tradition in the perspective of world culture.

Three more points of affinity between Coomaraswamy and Tagore may be noted briefly. In the first place, their educational writings reveal a close affinity of outlook. In their criticism of the educational system established by the British in India, in their plea for a positive reappraisal of the ancient ideals and methods of Indian education, in attaching great importance to simplicity of life and closeness to nature, and in insisting that education should not be merely intellectual but should also take into account the moral, emotional, and aesthetic sides of the learner's personality — in all these matters Tagore and Coomaraswamy often expressed almost identical views. Secondly, Coomaraswamy and Tagore were among the first thinkers of the modern age in India to emphasize the extent and depth of Buddhist influence on Indian culture. Many of

Tagore's poems, plays, letters and travel-journals show the deep influence of the Buddha's personality and teachings. Coomaraswamy's books on Buddhism and his comparative exposition of Hinduism and Buddhism gave a new direction to philosophical and religious studies. Coomaraswamy and Tagore took the initiative in removing two prevalent misconceptions about Buddhism: that it is pessimistic and nihilistic; and that it rejects the basic doctrines of Hinduism, especially the concept of the Self. Finally, Coomaraswamy and Tagore should together be given credit for drawing attention to the folk elements in India's cultural evolution. Coomaraswamy's studies of folk art and of the myths and symbols of primitive religion showed the close relationship between the classical and the popular modes of creative expression, and even metaphysical speculation, in the Indian tradition. The same result was achieved by Tagore's writings on popular proverbs and sayings, music, and poetry.

In some ways, however, Coomaraswamy was closer in spirit to Gandhi than to Tagore. He saw in Gandhi a more authentic representative of the orthodox tradition. While Tagore's religion had an element of eclecticism, Coomaraswamy looked upon the Gandhian way of life as a direct expression of the best in Hinduism (which, in his judgment, had assimilated and digested all that was valuable in Buddhism). Gandhi was a stern critic of modern industrial society and asserted that India had nothing to gain from Western technology, which flourished in proportion to the multiplication of wants. On this question, Coomaraswamy seems to have been in almost complete agreement with him. Tagore was a little more willing to see the positive side of technology and on several occasions dissociated himself from Gandhi's outright condemnation of it.

Coomaraswamy, like Mahatma Gandhi, accepted the social philosophy on which the fourfold division of society — the *Varnashrama Dharma* — was originally based. Both were convinced that the caste system, in its present form, did not reflect the ancient social ideals which were fundamentally sound. Gandhi waged a heroic struggle against caste discrimination and oppression and risked his very life in the movement against "untouchability." But he repeatedly declared that he was not against the concept of caste as such. Rabindranath Tagore, on the contrary, rejected the caste system outright and was not impressed by the philosophical justifications offered on its behalf.

Two final points may be mentioned in showing how Coomaraswamy differed from Gandhi. First, he did not share Gandhi's admiration for the parliamentary system of government. Both of them glorified the ancient ideal of a state based on Dharma. But Gandhi was convinced that in the modern age India must accept parliamentary democracy, while continuing to derive inspiration from the ideal of *Rama Rajya.* Coomaraswamy had grave misgivings about what he termed the "tyranny of the majority." Secondly, Coomaraswamy could not accept Gandhi's puritanical views on art. "Gandhi can be looked upon as a moral saint," Coomaraswamy once remarked, "but not as an aesthetic saint. He said, for instance, that a woman should not wear a necklace. Had he also been an aesthetic saint he would have said that if a woman wore a necklace it should be a good one!"[1]

II   *Concluding Review*

Coomaraswamy's reputation as a scholar, which was already secure in his lifetime, stands even higher today in the light of his posthumous publications and better understanding of the value of his researches. He adopted very exacting criteria of intellectual integrity, meticulous attention to detail, and strict adherence to the principle that no assertion be made without the sanction of primary sources. Here and there in his writings we come across terms and names that have become obsolete. For instance, he refers to Ceylon and Siam while today the names Shri Laṅkā and Thailand would be preferred. Similarly we find him using Brahmanism and Muhammadanism instead of Hinduism and Islam; and sometimes he uses the term *Hinayana* rather than *Theravada,* which is now current. But apart from these minor changes, there is hardly anything in his voluminous writings which would need revision from a purely scholarly point of view three decades after his death.

But to what extent, it might be asked, have his opinions and interpretations stood the test of time? Before attempting to answer this question one important point should be remembered. In a certain specific situation a strong, vehement statement may become necessary, even if subsequently it has to be toned down. Engels, the collaborator of Karl Marx, once conceded that they had probably overestimated the importance of economic factors in history. But he added that these factors had been grossly underestimated and sometimes altogether ignored in the past; therefore it was necessary to correct the balance. Similarly, we may find in Ananda Coomara-

swamy's writings some passages which seem to give a wholly negative picture of modern Western civilization, and others in which the
life and culture of traditional societies has received nothing but
praise. But it should be remembered that, at the time when he was
writing, it had become customary to dub all traditional cultures as
stagnant and out-of-date. The very word *tradition* evoked the scorn
of most Westerners. On the other hand, the euphoria created by
scientific inventions had made people oblivious of the dangers of
modern industrialism. Coomaraswamy's writings helped in correct-
ing the balance.

I am not suggesting that we should abstain from criticizing the
exaggerations which we sometimes find in Coomaraswamy. For
instance, when he says that modern technological civilizations "can
be likened to a headless corpse whose last motions are convulsive
and insignificant," we have a right to object that the elements of
strength derived from scientific progress have not been recognized.
When he asserts that "a philosophy identical with Plato's is still a
living force in the East," we cannot help feeling that the persistence
and continuity of the metaphysical tradition in the actual life of the
Indian people has been exaggerated. His belief that "the education
of the Indian peasant and the Indian woman is already admirable,
... and none of us are qualified to improve it"[2] will not be easily
shared by those familiar with the realities of the Indian situation.
The statement that "India is today a land of cultivated peasants
and uncultivated leaders" may appear as less than fair to the pioneers of Indian nationalism who, though Western-educated, had
their feet firmly planted in the traditional culture of their land.

A few such overstatements, however, do not in any way affect
the total value of Coomaraswamy's work. The discriminating student will note them and question their validity; but he will not let
them interfere with his enjoyment of and admiration for Coomaraswamy's writings. The "Doctor," as he was affectionaly called by
his friends, had a clear, unambiguous aim: to discover the roots of
all that is of abiding value in man's inner life and in the creative
expression of that life. He pursued this aim for nearly half a century with undiminished vigor and zest. In this process he sometimes
saw, with deep anguish, the destruction of much that was noble and
beautiful through modern man's egoism and insensitiveness.
Speaking of Rajput painting, he once said, "This is the only visible
record of a world of wonder and beauty that is passing away before
our very eyes, unrecognized and unregretted."[3] In another context

he said, "The beauty and logic of Indian life belong to a dying past. The nineteenth century has degraded much and created nothing."[4] Such expressions of pessimism are, however, rare in his writings. He had a strong faith in the survival value of the perennial philosophy, and his researches sustained that faith by bringing to light the persistence of the traditional way of life in so-called backward societies.

Coomaraswamy's lifelong endeavor was to remove the prejudices which prevented scholars — particularly in the West — from appreciating life-styles other than those which they had assumed to be 'natural" in the modern world. "We must realize," he said, "that others have sought their images... not as we seek them, outside of ourselves, but in their own hearts. These men lived in a world which we know less than the Antarctic or the frozen north — a world perhaps more real and more wonderful than ours.... We should give thanks to them for showing us that our world is no absolute *ding an sich,* and that the shadows of reality are of many varied outlines and move across our vision with mysterious elusiveness. Perhaps the greatest art is to show that no one shadow is eternal or self-existent: only Light is that."[5]

Few men in the modern age have practiced with such skill and devotion this greatest of all arts — the art of perceiving the one light that endures through the transient shadows.

Notes and References

Chapter One

1. Professor Norman Brown, in a tribute quoted in *Remembering and Remembering Again and Again* (Edited by S. Durai Raja Singam and published by him from Petaling Jaya, Malaysia, 1974. This book will be referred to as RRAA throughout the references that follow.)

2. Cf. Upanishad: "He falls into deep darkness who follows the path of ignorance. But he falls into still deeper darkness who follows the path of knowledge." Coomaraswamy, in conformity with the Upanishad tradition, rejects conceptual knowledge as an end in itself.

3. Margaret Marcus, *Ananda, the Blessed One, Was a Presence That is Hard to be Without.* (RRAA, p. 35.)

4. The name Shri Lankā, rather than Ceylon, has been used in this work, and in the References, except in quotations.

5. This point has been stressed by Curt F. Leidecker, who says, "He was too encyclopedic a mind that any casual student could do justice to his genius. More than study, his work requires insight. Hence it is amusing to see people whom he criticized, let us say in a book review, come back at him with inane remarks and extenuations totally beside the point."

6. Ram Mohan Roy, founder of the Brahma Samaj, was born in 1772 and died in 1833.

7. Swami Vivekananda (1863-1902), the foremost disciple of Shri Ramakrishna, was the first to present Vedanta Philosophy to Western audiences at the Parliament of Religions at Chicago (1894).

8. Sarvepalli Radhakrishnan (1888-1974) lectured on Indian Philosophy at Oxford. Among his writings, in which the Indian point of view in philosophy and religion has been forcefully expressed, the following are especially important: *East and West, An Idealist View of Life, Eastern Religions and Western Thought* and *Kalki, or the Future of Civilization.*

9. Rabindranath Tagore's lectures in England and America were published by Macmillan and Co. in two volumes: *Sadhana, or the Realisation of Life,* and *Creative Unity.*

10. Dogmatism is often seen in the formulations: India is spiritualistic, while the West is materialistic; and the dark side of Indian life exists only in the distortions of Western writers. At the other extreme are the apologists who argue as follows: "It is true that we are backward, irrational, superstitious, etc. But we were not always like this. Give us a chance. We

may yet improve." Coomaraswamy has condemned both these attitudes in various contexts.

11. The sectarians count among their ranks many prominent historians who belittle or ignore the contribution made by the Muslims to Indian culture. Partisanship is also seen in neglecting the pre-Aryan element in Indian culture or — at the other extreme — exaggerating it out of all proportion.

12. This metaphor is used by Tagore in many of his esays and poems.

13. Coomaraswamy's interest in medieval Indian culture is seen in his studies of Mughal and Rajput painting, religious movements, and theistic poetry in many Indian languages of the North as well as the South. As for modern India, his close observation of trends in art and poetry are seen in his studies of the Bengal School of Art and of Tagore's poetry, music, and painting.

14. In an address on *Education in Ceylon,* Coomaraswamy said, "The more I know of Ceylon, the more inseparable from India does it appear, and I sometimes regret that they are not under one administration. If we are to attain the liberty of spirit which is the true end of education, if we would recover our lost character as orientals, we must turn to India and base our education on Indian ideals." *Art and Swadeshi,* p. 149.

15. His feelings are summed up in his message on the day of India's attainment of independence: "Be yourself!"

16. To mention only a few examples, Coomaraswamy had nothing but praise for Eric Gill, Rene Guenon, Marco Pallis, E. B. Havell, and Romain Rolland.

17. Coomaraswamy points out in many of his essays that the concept of the White Man's Burden, openly asserted by Macaulay and Kipling, is reflected in a subtle — and therefore more dangerous — form in the work of many Western anthropologists and social psychologists. Instead of crudely labelling oriental societies as inferior, these scientists speak of "potentially excellent people, just waiting for the liberating touch of modern science."

18. Coomaraswamy refers to ancient Indian universities like Nālandā and Vikramshila, where the concept of international brotherhood was made the foundation of education centuries before any Western educators thought along these lines.

19. Jacques de Marquette refers to Coomaraswamy's important contribution in "exploding the dangerous fallacy" of some modern psychoanalysts "who assert the existence of a radical difference, and even opposition, between the 'racial sub-conscious' of different branches of the human family." (*An Appreciation.* RRAA, p. 16.)

20. No names need be mentioned: one has only to see the pretensions, lifestyles, and modes of behavior of the leaders of some of the contemporary "spiritual" cults to realize how little they have in common with the traditional concept of the Teacher-Sage.

21. Coomaraswamy gives several instances of mystification resulting from the use of scientific jargon, based on the vocabulary of physics and mathematics.

22. Until the forties of this century, children in many Indian schools were taught that India groped in darkness for a thousand years and was exposed to the light of reason only when English education was introduced in Bengal at the end of the eighteenth century.

23. Cf. Rabindranath Tagore: "The doctrine of the Buddha has generated two divergent currents of thought: the one impersonal, preaching abnegation of the self through discipline; and the other personal, preaching the cultivation of sympathy for all creatures and devotion to the infinite truth of love. The latter, represented by the Mahāyāna, had its origin in the positive aspect of the Buddha's teaching, which is immeasurable Love. It could never, by any logic, find its reality in the emptiness of the truthless abyss."

24. Shunyavada, literally "Doctrine of Emptiness," was developed by Nagarjuna, who repeatedly asserts that it is *not* Nihilism. The doctrine is, in fact, known as *Mādhyamika Darshana* (The Philosophy of the Middle Way) because it rejects two extreme views: "that everything exists" and "that nothing exists."

25. The emergence of Mahāyāna as the dominant trend in Buddhism shows that "Bhakti" in the Buddhist tradition is also at least as old as the first century B.C. Coomaraswamy emphasizes that the "Way of Devotion" is recognized by all the major Indian religious traditions: Hindu, Buddhist, Jaina, and Islamic.

26. Cf. Coomaraswamy's comments on Mughal and Rajput painting quoted in Chapter III of this book.

27. M. S. Randhava, in his essay on *Rediscovery of Kāngrā Painting,* explains in detail the importance of Coomaraswamy's contribution to the study of this school of art. (RRAA, pp. 201-204.)

Chapter Two

1. It is interesting to note that Ananda Coomaraswamy found a copper figurine of Kumāra in the bed of the Kalu Ganga river in the Ratnapura District of Shri Lankā. The figurine is now in the Colombo Museum.

2. The poem, which has been translated into English, is entitled "The Birth of the War-God."

3. Cf. S. Durai Raja Singam: *The Life and Writings of Sir Mutu Coomaraswamy.*

4. Ananda, literally "Joy," is obviously a symbolic name in the Buddha legend, suggesting that Joy is Buddha's constant companion (in spite of his stress on the universality of suffering).

5. For details of Coomaraswamy's boyhood days at Wycliffe School

see *Memories of Classmates* (RRAA, pp. 245-248.)

6. The first published work of Coomaraswamy is an essay on a geological subject: "A Note on the Occurrence of Corundum as a Contact-Mineral at Pont Paul near Morlaix," *Quarterly Journal of the Geological Society,* LVII, 185-188).

7. The Theosophical Society was founded by Madame Blavatsky and Colonel Olcott in 1876. It was under the leadership of Mrs. Annie Besant that the Theosophical movement became an important force among urban intellectuals in India. The Theosophists still meet in small groups and the Theosophical Society publishes books on religious themes. The most enduring contribution of this movement has been in the field of education, especially at the elementary and Middle School level.

8. Abanindranath made a pencil sketch of Coomaraswamy in 1908 and painted a portrait in watercolor in 1910. For a description of these, see Dinkar Koushik, "Abanindranath: A Review, *Vishvabharati Quarterly,* Vol. 37, No. 3-4.

9. The refusal of the Government of India to accept Coomaraswamy's collection has been looked upon as a great national loss. Undoubtedly, the collection would have been in India today if a foreign government had not been in power at that time. However, Coomaraswamy's splendid work at the Boston Museum has compensated for the loss.

10. Philosophically, Ashbee's views may be described as a kind of quasi-socialism with overtones of Rousseau's "back-to-nature" approach.

11. Quoted from Ashbee's journal of October, 1914.

12. Coomaraswamy and Eric Gill kept in touch with each other through common friends, especially Bernard Kelly and Walter Shewring. (See the latter's "Ananda Coomaraswamy and Eric Gill" in RRAA, pp. 189-190.)

13. Dr. Denman Ross was born in 1853. He inherited a large fortune, which he spent in extensive travels and in collecting works of oriental art. He was elected to the Board of Trustees of the Boston Museum in 1895.

14. Speaking at the flag-hoisting ceremony at Harvard on August 15, 1947, Coomaraswamy said, "I am proud of a nation whose flag is not nationalistic but points to man's relation with the cosmos."

15. Coomaraswamy's son, Rama, traveled in the company of the famous scholar Marco Pallis, author of *Peaks and Lamas.*

16. Quoted by James Marshall Plumer in *The Farewell Dinner* (RRAA, pp. 275-276.)

17. For a description of Coomaraswamy's last hours, see Robert Winzer Bruce: *The Ninth of September* in RRAA, p. 283.

18. Patrick A. Moore, who accompanied Mrs. Coomaraswamy to the confluence of the Ganges and the Jumna at Allahabad for the immersion of Coomaraswamy's ashes, has given an account of the event. (RRAA, p. 287.)

19. Letter to Durai Raja Singam, written from Boston some time in May, 1946.

20. For Durai Raja Singam's contribution to Coomaraswamiana see the Preface to this book.

21. The remark is attributed to Coomaraswamy's wife, Dona Luisa.

22. For a description of Coomaraswamy's home see *Keeper of the Indian Section: An Appreciation,* by Ardelia Ripley Hall. (RRAA, pp. 106-123.)

23. *Ibid.,* p. 116.

24. Ashton Sanborn in *Memories of Colleagues* (RRAA, p. 160.)

25. Lucian de Silva in *Memories from Classmates* (RRAA, p. 248.)

26. Richard G. Salomon in *Unique Mediator Between the Worlds of Indian Thought and Western Scholarship* (RRAA, p. 238.)

27. Mayo Johnson and other friends of the Coomaraswamys were told about the latter's decision to settle in India. (See RRAA, p. 298.)

28. The metaphor of the salmon returning to the source (the finite returning to the infinite) is reminiscent of Tagore's symbolism of the swan returning to his Himalayan home.

Chapter Three

1. Quoted by Ralph Allerton Parker in his Preface to Coomaraswamy's *Bugbear of Literacy.*

2. "Mahatma," contributed to *Mahatma Gandhi: Essays and Reflections on His Life and Work,* edited by S. Radhakrishnan. London: George Allen & Unwin, 1939.

3. Robert Ulich: "Memorial Service at Funeral," September 9, 1947. (RRAA, pp. 284-286.)

4. Robert Allerton Parker: Preface to *Bugbear of Literacy.*

5. Cf. the Hindi proverb: "Gagar men sagar bharna."

6. Cf. B. N. Goswami: "Ananda Coomaraswamy as Historian of Rajput Painting." (RRAA, p. 75.)

7. This remark should be seen in the context of Coomaraswamy's view that folk art is rooted in certain metaphysical assumptions of the perennial philosophy.

8. *Hinduism and Buddhism,* p. 3.

9. "Swadeshi, True and False," from *Art and Swadeshi,* pp. 11-12.

10. *Art and Swadeshi,* p. 72.

11. *Ibid.,* p. 90.

12. See comments on a miniature painting, "The Bride" in *Art and Swadeshi,* p. 92.

13. *Dance of Shiva* (from book of the same title) p. 78.

14. Christmas Humphreys, founder of the British Buddhist Society, and A. L. Basham, author of the well-known work *The Wonder That Was India,* were among those influenced by this book.

15. "Early Indian Architecture" (Part I: *Cities and Gates;* Part II: "Bodhigrihas" published in *Eastern Art,* II, 208-235.)

16. "Early Indian Iconography." Part I published in *Eastern Art*, I, 32-41; Part II in *Eastern Art*, I, 174-189.

17. For instance, "A Chinese Buddhist Water-Vessel and Its Proto-type" in *Artibus Asiae*, II, 122-143.

18. Romain Rolland's Introduction is not included in the paperback edition of *Dance of Shiva*. It is included in the hard-cover published by Asia Publishing House, Bombay, 1948.

19. "Cosmopolitanism of Nietzsche," *Dance of Shiva*, p. 147.

20. "Young India," *Dance of Shiva*, p. 162.

21. *History of Indian and Indonesian Art*, p. 158.

22. *Ibid.*, p. 128.

23. *Yakshas*, Part I, p. 14.

24. "Theory of Art in Asia," *Transformation of Nature in Art*, p. 3.

25. *Christian and Oriental Philosophy of Art*, p. 89.

26. *Hinduism and Buddhism*, p. 15.

27. *Ibid.*, p. 19.

28. *Ibid.*, p. 25.

29. *Ibid.*, p. 51.

30. *Ibid.*, p. 74.

31. *Bugbear of Literacy*, p. 37.

32. *Ibid.*, p. 38.

33. *Ibid.*, p. 10.

34. *Ibid.*, p. 13.

35. *Ibid.*, p. 79.

36. *Ibid.*, p. 70.

37. *Ibid.*, p. 59.

38. *Ibid.*, p. 100.

Chapter Four

1. James Marshall Plumer, "The Farewell Dinner." (RRAA, p. 274.)

2. When Coomaraswamy speaks of views "which I have made my own" he expresses the traditional Indian assumption that the acceptance of ideas involves personal commitment no less than intellectual conviction.

3. From Coomaraswamy's speech at the farewell dinner at the Harvard Club, August 22, 1947.

4. *Christian and Oriental Philosophy of Art*, p. 22.

5. The Bibliography was published in the journal *Ars Islamica*, 1942, 125.

6. *Hinduism and Buddhism*, p. 45.

7. *Bugbear of Literacy*, p. 12.

8. *Ibid.*, p. 69.

9. *Ibid.*, p. 70.

10. "East and West" from *Bugbear of Literacy*, p. 11.

11. *Bugbear of Literacy,* p. 79.

12. The metaphor of people speaking about the same thing in different languages occurs frequently in the parables of Shri Ramakrishna.

13. "Intellectual Fraternity," *Dance of Shiva,* p. 136.

14. *Ibid.,* p. 136.

15. St. Augustine, *Confessions,* IX, 10.

16. Quoted in "Hindu View of Art: Historical," *Dance of Shiva,* p. 28.

17. Quoted in "Intellectual Fraternity," *Dance of Shiva,* p. 136.

18. "Pertinence of Philosophy," in *Contemporary Indian Philosophy,* edited by S. Radhakrishnan and J. H. Muirhead. London: George Allen and Unwin, p. 152.

19. *Ibid.,* p. 153.

20. *Ibid.,* p. 154.

21. *Ibid.,* p. 156.

22. "Paths That Lead to the Same Summit," *Bugbear of Literacy,* p. 60.

23. "Eastern Wisdom and Western Knowledge," *Bugbear of Literacy,* p. 69.

24. *The Gospel of Shri Ramakrishna* is the English version of Ramakrishna's conversations recorded in Bengali by one of his disciples who signed only his initial 'M.'

25. Aldous Huxley: *The Perennial Philosophy.* New York: Harper Colophon Books, 1944, p. vii.

26. *Ibid.,* p. vii.

27. *Ibid.,* p. xi.

28. Recalling a conversation with Coomaraswamy, Whitall N. Perry says, "I asked if his doctrinal perspective corresponded with that of Rene Guenon. He said it did essentially, that they were entirely in agreement on metaphysical principles, although there were minor divergences on one or two subordinate points." "The Man and the Witness" in RRAA, p. 5.

29. "Eastern Wisdom and Western Knowledge" (in a review of Guenon's "East and West"). *Bugbear of Literacy,* p. 70.

30. "Am I My Brother's Keeper?" *Bugbear of Literacy,* p. 11.

31. Gai Eaton: "Two Traditionalists," RRAA, p. 340.

32. *Ibid.,* p. 343.

33. Whitall N. Perry: "The Man and the Witness," RRAA, p. 7.

34. "Pertinence of Philosophy," *op. cit.,* p. 156.

35. *Ibid.,* p. 159.

36. *Ibid.*

37. *Ibid.,* p. 157.

38. *Ibid.,* p. 160.

39. *Hinduism and Buddhism,* p. 10.

40. "Origin and Use of Images in India," *Transformation of Nature in Art,* p. 158.

41. *Hinduism and Buddhism,* p. 11.

42. *Ibid.,* p. 43.

43. "Origin and Use of Images in India," *Transformation of Nature in Art,* p. 161.

44. *Ibid.,* p. 160.

45. *Ibid.,* p. 161.

46. Cf. Meister Eckhart: "Yonder no work is done at all."

47. *Hinduism and Buddhism,* p. 59.

48. Cf. *Lankāvatāra Sutra* (a text frequently referred to by Zen masters), where the Self, "realized within ourselves in absolute purity," is identified with the *Tathāgatagarbha.*

49. "Pertinence of Philosophy," *op. cit.,* p. 169.

50. *Ibid.,* p. 171.

51. The Ideal of the Bodhisatva, Coomaraswamy points out, is essentially the same as the Hindu and Sufi ideals referred to here.

52. "Pertinence of Philosophy," *op. cit.,* p. 161.

53. *Ibid.*

54. *Ibid.,* p. 162.

55. *Ibid.*

56. *Ibid.,* p. 164.

57. *Time and Eternity.* Quoted by Whitall N. Perry in "The Man and the Witness," RRAA, p. 3.

58. "Pertinence of Philosophy," *op. cit.,* p. 171.

59. The Real (*sat*) is the same as the Imperishable (*amrita*). Thus Immortality is not an attribute of Reality (among other attributes): the two are identical.

60. "Indian Music," *Dance of Shiva,* p. 96.

61. This point is elaborated by Coomaraswamy in his essay "The One and Only Transmigrant," *Review of Religion,* (March 1946) Vol. X, No. 3.

62. Also quoted by Aldous Huxley in his *Perennial Philosophy, op. cit.,* p. 213.

63. "What Has India Contributed to Human Welfare?" *Dance of Shiva,* p. 10.

64. *Hinduism and Buddhism,* pp. 28-29.

65. *Ibid.,* p. 66.

66. *Ibid.,* p. 67.

67. "Cosmopolitanism of Nietzsche," *Dance of Shiva,* p. 141.

68. *Ibid.,* p. 144.

69. *Ibid.,* p. 146.

Chapter Five

1. *Christian and Oriental Philosophy of Art,* p. 23.

2. *Ibid.,* p. 3 (from "Why Exhibit Works of Art?").

3. *Ibid.,* p. 25.

4. *Ibid.*, p. 12.

5. *Ibid.*, p. 84 (from "Is Art a Superstition or a Way of Life?").

6. *Ibid.*, p. 92 (from "What is the Use of Art, Anyway?").

7. *Ibid.*, p. 46.

8. Quoted by Bernard Bosanquet in "A History of Aesthetic."

9. Coomaraswamy is, obviously, not disputing the fact that an aesthetic response to an object or an idea is qualitatively different from other types of response. His objection is to the use of this term by a person who really means that he is deriving a pleasurable sensation.

10. Quoted from "Art and Life in New Guinea" by R. Firth.

11. *Christian and Oriental Philosophy of Art,* p. 30.

12. *Ibid.,* p. 25.

13. *Ibid.*, p. 91 (from "What is the Use of Art, Anyway?").

14. "Meister Eckhart's View of Art," *Transformation of Nature in Art,* pp. 64-65.

15. "Why Exhibit Works of Art?" *Christian and Oriental Philosophy of Art,* p. 15.

16. *Ibid.*

17. *Ibid.*

18. Cf. St. Thomas: "The artist works by art and willingly" (per artem et ex voluntate). Quoted by Coomaraswamy in *Christian and Oriental Philosophy of Art,* p. 24.

19. *Bhagavadgītā*, XVIII, 45.

20. "What is the Use of Art, Anyway?" *op. cit.,* p. 92.

21. "Why Exhibit Works of Art?" p. 22.

22. Coomaraswamy's criticism of the commercialization of art in capitalist society is similar to that of Karl Marx. Cf. Dale Riepe's essay on this theme in RRAA, pp. 99-105.

23. "Why Exhibit Works of Art?" p. 9.

24. In this context Coomaraswamy also refers to Dewey's criticism of the "snobbishness" of modern cultural attitudes.

25. Coomaraswamy emphasizes that traditional art is close to religion because the latter, too, combines the utilitarian and the ideological sides of life. Here the word "utilitarian" must not be taken as "functional" in the narrow sense.

26. Cf. *Kaushītakī Upanishad* where the sensational and the intelligible elements of appearance are distinguished and it is asserted that "truly, from either alone no aspect whatever could be produced." (Quoted by Coomaraswamy in *Transformation of Nature in Art,* p. 14.)

27. *Christian and Oriental Philosophy of Art,* (title essay) p. 31.

28. "Is Art a Superstition or a Way of Life?" p. 64.

29. *Ibid.,* p. 65.

30. *Ibid.*

31. *Ibid.,* (title essay) p. 32.

32. Quoted in "Hindu View of Art: Historical," *Dance of Shiva,* p. 24.

33. "I take refuge in the Buddha. I take refuge in the Dharma. I take refuge in the Samgha."

34. "Hindu View of Art: Historical," p. 25.

35. "Why Exhibit Works of Art?" p. 16.

36. *Ibid.*, p. 22.

37. The passage from Plato's *Republic* is reproduced from Carritt's *The Philosophies of Beauty*.

38. Quoted by Coomaraswamy in his References to *Christian and Oriental Philosophy of Art*. Reference no. 21, p. 54.

39. *Ibid.*, p. 40.

40. *Ibid.*, p. 25.

41. *Ibid.*

42. Some modern writers refers to the *characteristic* as the *unique*. Whatever the term used, the individualism typical of the modern West is always evident.

43. "Is Art a Superstition or a Way of Life?" p. 61.

44. *Christian and Oriental Philosophy of Art,* (title essay) p. 39.

45. *Ibid.*, p. 40.

46. *Bhagavadgītā:* III, 27.

47. *Christian and Oriental Philosophy of Art,* (title essay), p. 52.

48. *Ibid.*, p. 39.

49. *Ibid.*, p. 38.

50. *Ibid.*, p. 35.

51. *Ibid.*

52. *Ibid.*, p. 36.

53. *Ibid.*, p. 54.

54. "Theory of Art in Asia," *Transformation of Nature in Art,* p. 23.

55. "Is Art a Superstition or a Way of Life?" p. 68.

56. It may be noted that since Coomaraswamy wrote this essay, the craze for novelty — culminating in the glorification of "strangeness" as something intrinsically valuable — has assumed disturbing proportions in every field of culture in the West.

57. "Is Art a Superstition or a Way of Life?" p. 72.

58. Also cf. "Styles are the accident, by no means the essence of art; the free man is not trying to express himself but that which was to be expressed." *Christian and Oriental Philosophy of Art.* (Title essay), p. 39.

59. "Is Art a Superstition or a Way of Life?" p. 70.

60. *Ibid.*, p. 70.

61. *Ibid.*, p. 71.

62. *Ibid.*

63. Sometimes Coomaraswamy uses even stronger words. The plagiarist is described as being no better than a forger.

64. "Is Art a Superstition or a Way of Life?," p. 71.

65. From this point of view, Coomaraswamy asserts, the art of the American Indian sand-painter is superior in kind to any painting done in

Europe or white America within the last several centuries.

66. *Christian and Oriental Philosophy of Art*, (title essay), p. 24

67. "What is the Use of Art, Anyway?" p. 99.

68. *Ibid.*, pp. 98-99.

69. *Christian and Oriental Philosophy of Art*, (title essay), p. 38

70. *Ibid.*, p. 38-39.

71. Cf. the idea of "self-naughting" discussed in Chapter IV above.

72. "Why Exhibit Works of Art?" p. 19.

73. *Ibid.*

74. Plato says that art serves to attune our thought to cosmic harmonies "so that by an assimilation of the knower to the to-be-known, the archetypal nature, and coming to be in that likeness, we may attain at last to a part in that 'life's best' that has been appointed by the gods to man for this time being and hereafter." (Quoted by Coomaraswamy in "Why Exhibit Works of Art?")

75. For instance in *Aitareya Brahmana,* VI, 27 (Quoted by Coomaraswamy in *Transformation of Nature in Art*, p. 8.)

76. *Christian and Oriental Philosophy of Art*, (title essay), p. 44

77. Quoted in "Indian Music," *Dance of Shiva*, p. 95.

78. *Ibid.*, p. 94.

79. *Christian and Oriental Philosophy of Art,* (title essay), p. 44.

80. *Ibid.*

81. For the religious basis of architecture, cf. Coomaraswamy's essay: "Symbolism of the Dome."

82. Tamil version, quoted by Kearns in *Indian Antiquary,* Vol V (1876).

83. Quoted in "Hindu View of Art: Historical," *Dance of Shiva,* p. 31.

84. Coomaraswamy describes this as "guild socialism in a noncompetitive society."

85. "Theory of Art in Asia," *Transformation of Nature in Art*, p. 5.

86. *Mālavikāgnimitra:* II:2. (Quoted in "Theory of Art in Asia.")

87. *Shukranītisāra:* IV, 7, 73.

88. It is significant that in the Buddha's "Eightfold Way," as in Patanjali's *Yogasutra,* the last item mentioned is *samādhi.*

89. Here, again, the point being made is that contemplation is not a passive state.

90. Samkara's commentary on the *Brahma Sūtras,* III, ii, 10.

91. Quoted in "Hindu View of Art: Historical," *Dance of Shiva,* p. 26.

92. Quoted in "Aesthetics of the *Shukranītisāra*" *Transformation of Nature in Art,* pp. 113ff.

93. Quoted in "Hindu View of Art: Historical," *Dance of Shiva,* p. 27.

94. *Ibid.*, p. 28.

95. Quoted in "Hindu View of Art: Historical," p. 27.

96. This is a common simile in Indian literature. The Buddha is described as having seen Liberation "like a fruit on the palm of my right hand."

97. Quoted in "Hindu View of Art: Historical," *Dance of Shiva*, p.29.
98. *Ibid.,* p. 28.
99. *Ibid.,* p. 29.
100. *Ibid.,* pp. 29-30.
101. *Transformation of Nature in Art,* p. 8.
102. *Ibid.*
103. *Ibid.,* p. 10.
104. *Ibid.,* p. 12.
105. *Ibid.*
106. *Ibid.,* p. 11.
107. *Ibid.,* p. 13.
108. *Ibid.,* p. 14.
109. *Ibid.,* p. 13.
110. *Ibid., p. 29.*
111. *Ibid.*
112. *Ibid.,* p. 4.
113. *Christian and Oriental Philosophy of Art,* p. 28.
114. *Dance of Shiva,* p. 42.
115. Quoted by Coomaraswamy from Millet. (*Dance of Shiva*, p. 47.)
116. *Ibid.,* p. 52.
117. *Christian and Oriental Philosophy of Art,* p. 77.
118. *Ibid.*
119. *Dance of Shiva,* p. 37.
120. *Ibid.,* p. 41.
121. Quoted by Coomraswamy in *Dance of Shiva,* p. 41.
122. *Dance of Shiva,* p. 41.

Chapter Six

1. *Dance of Shiva,* p. 21.
2. *Ibid.,* p. 4.
3. *Ibid.,* p. 5.
4. *Hinduism and Buddhism,* p. 26.
5. *Ibid.,* p. 27.
6. *Ibid.*
7. "What Has India Contributed to Human Welfare?" *Dance of Shiva,* p. 15.
8. *Ibid.,* p. 15.
9. *Ibid.,* p. 10.
10. *Ibid.,* p. 17.
11. "East and West," from *The Bugbear of Literacy,* p. 82.
12. "What Has India Contributed to Human Welfare?" *op. cit.,* p. 5.
13. Quoted in *Dance of Shiva,* p. 8.
14. "What Has India Contributed to Human Welfare?" *op. cit.,* p. 6.

15. "Individuality, Autonomy, and Function," from *The Dance of Shiva*, p. 168.

16. This line is taken from an oft-quoted Upanishadic stanza.

17. "Individuality, Autonomy, and Function," *op. cit.*, p. 170.

18. *Ibid.*, p. 171.

19. *Art and Swadeshi*, p. 111.

20. *Ibid.*, p. 112.

21. "Individuality, Autonomy, and Function," *op. cit.*, p. 166.

22. *Dance of Shiva*, p. 114. Cf. references to goddesses in *Myths of the Hindus and the Buddhists* by Ananda Coomaraswamy and Sister Nivedita.

23. *The Dance of Shiva*, p. 121.

24. *Ibid.*, p. 100.

25. *Ibid.*, p. 105.

26. For further comments on this theme, see Coomaraswamy's *Yakshas* and *History of Indian and Indonesian Art.*

27. Quoted in *Dance of Shiva*, p. 119.

28. *Ibid.*, p. 120.

29. *Ibid.*, p. 103.

30. *Ibid.*, p. 102.

31. This is humorously expressed in a Hindi adage which can be translated thus: "Look at that wife, walking humbly ten paces behind her husband. She has the bunch of keys!"

32. *Rajatarangini* ("The River of Kings") was composed by the poet-historian Kalhana in the twelfth century A.D. It is a chronicle of the kings of Kashmir.

33. "The Status of Women in India," in *Dance of Shiva*, p. 102.

34. *Ibid.*, p. 102.

35. *Ibid.*, p. 105.

36. *Ibid.*, p. 106.

37. "Young India," from *Dance of Shiva*, p. 154.

38. "The Status of Women in India," *op. cit.*, p. 120.

39. Coomaraswamy: "The Oriental View of Women" (essay made available through the courtesy of Mr. S. Durai Raja Singam).

40. "The Status of Women in India," *op. cit.*, p. 119.

41. *Ibid.*, p. 108.

42. *Ibid.*, p. 120.

43. *Ibid.*, p. 117.

44. "The Oriental View of Women."

45. "East and West," from *The Bugbear of Literacy*, p. 87.

46. "Young India," from *Dance of Shiva*, p. 156.

47. *Ibid.*

48. *Art and Swadeshi*, p. 54.

49. The reference is to Macaulay's famous (or notorious) "Minute on

Indian Education" outlining the British Government's educational policy in India.

50. *The Bugbear of Literacy*, p. 2.

51. *Art and Swadeshi*, p. 141.

52. *Ibid.*

53. *Ibid.*, p. 142.

54. Cf. Rabindranath Tagore's comments on this subject in his essays "My School" and "An Eastern University."

55. *Art and Swadeshi*, p. 144.

56. *The Dance of Shiva*, p. 9.

57. Quoted in *The Bugbear of Literacy*, p. 31.

58. *Art and Swadeshi*, p. 143.

59. *Ibid.*, p. 145.

60. *The Dance of Shiva*, p. 17.

Chapter Seven

1. Conversation with Dorothy Norman. Quoted by S. Durai Raja Singam in his article "Gandhiji and Ananda Coomaraswamy," *The Indian Reivew* (July, 1971).

2. *Art and Swadeshi*, p. 143.

3. *Ibid.*, p. 88.

4. *The Dance of Shiva*, p. 160.

5. *Art and Swadeshi*, p. 68.

Selected Bibliography

Note: In this bibliography, the writings of Ananda K. Coomaraswamy are listed in the chronological order of publication.

1900

"On Ceylon Rocks and Graphite." *Quarterly Journal of the Geological Society.* LVI, pp. 590-614. Figures: 4, Plates: XXIII.

1902

"The Crystalline Limestones of Ceylon." *Quarterly Journal of the Geological Society.* LVIII, pp. 399-402. Maps: 2.

1903-1905

Reports, Mineralogical Survey of Ceylon. Ceylon Administrative Reports. Colombo, Ceylon.

1905

"Notes on Paddy Cultivation Ceremonies in the Ratnapura District." *Royal Asiatic Society Journal,* Ceylon Branch, XVIII, No. 56, pp. 413–428.

1906

Handbook to the Exhibition of Arts and Crafts. (In connection with the *Ceylon Rubber Exhibition*) Colombo, Ceylon. Plates: 4.
"A Plea for the Teaching of Indian Music in Ceylon." *Journal of the Ceylon University Association.* Vol. I, No. 2, pp. 142–150.
"*Some Survivals in Simhalese Art.*" Ceylon Branch, *Royal Asiatic Society Journal,* XIX, No. 57. pp. 72–89.
"Kandyan Art: What It Meant And How It Ended." *Ceylon National Review,* January. Colombo, Ceylon.
"Two Kandyan Brass Boxes." *Ceylon National Review,* January, Colombo, Ceylon.
"Anglicisation of the East." (Presidential Address to the Ceylon Reform Society), *Ceylon National Review.* July. Colombo, Ceylon.

1907

"Notes on Painting, Dyeing, Lacework, Dumbara Mats and Paper in Ceylon," *Royal Asiatic Society Journal.* Ceylon Branch, XIX, No. 58, pp. 103–121.

The Deeper Meaning of the Struggle. Broad Campden, Englana: Essex House Press.

"Teaching of Drawing in Ceylon," *Ceylon National Review,* January. Colombo, Ceylon.

"India and Ceylon." *Ceylon National Review,* July. Columbo, Ceylon.

1908

Message of the East. Madras: Ganesh and Co.

Voluspa. Kandy, Ceylon.

The Aims of Indian Art. Broad Campden, England: Essex House Press.

"Vegetarianism in Ceylon." *Ceylon National Review,* 125-131, Columbo, Ceylon.

"Art of the East and the West." *Ceylon National Review,* VI, 229-233, Columbo, Ceylon.

"The Village Community and Modern Progress." *Ceylon National Review,* VII, 249-260, Columbo, Ceylon.

Medieval Simhalese Art: Being a Monograph on Medieval Simhalese Arts and Crafts mainly as surviving in the Eighteenth Century, with an account of the Structure of Society and the Status of the Craftsman. Broad Campden, England: Essex House Press.

The Influence of Greek on Indian Art. (Read at the 15th International Oriental Congress, Copenhagen, August 1908.) Broad Campden, England: Essex House Press.

1909

Essays in National Idealism. Colombo: Apothecaries Co. Also published by G. A. Natesan and Co., Madras (popular edition).

The Indian Craftsman. London: Probasthain.

"Evolution of Music in East and West." *Journal of the Ceylon University Association.* Vol. II, No. 7, pp. 178-191.

"Mahayana Buddhist Images from Ceylon and Java." *Journal of the Royal Asiatic Society,* 1908, pp. 283-297.

1910

Art and Swadeshi. Madras: Ganesh and Co.

Domestic Handicraft and Culture. Broad Campden, England: Essex House Press.

Indian Drawings. London: India Society.

Selected Examples of Indian Art. Broad Campden, England: Essex House Press.

The Oriental View of Women. (Originally appeared in *Votes for Women*) Broad Campden, England: Essex House Press.

"Originality in Mughal Painting." *Journal of the Royal Asiatic Society,* 1910, pp. 283-297 and 875-881.

"Indian Bronzes." *Burlington Magazine.* Vol. XVII, No. LXXXVI, pp. 86-94.

1912

Indian Drawings. (Second Series). London: India Society.
Burning and Melting (TR.) Being the *Suz-i-Gudaz* of Muhammad Raza Nau'i. (In collaboration with Mirza Y. Dawood) London: Old Bourne Press.
"Rajput Paintings." *Burlington Magazine.* Vol. XX, No. CVIII, pp. 315–324.

1913

"Sati: A Vindication of Hindu Women." *Sociological Review.* VI, pp. 117–135.
Some Ancient Elements in Indian Decorative Art. Ostasiatische Zeitschr, II, pages 383–392.
From the Psalms of Tayumana Swami, Prabuddha Bharata, Vol. XVIII No. 203 (June, p. 114) and No. 209 (December, pp. 234–236).
Indian Images With Many Arms, The Burlington Magazine, No. CXVIII, Vol. XXII, pp. 189–196.
Dr. R. F. Martin and Oriental Painting, The Burlington Magazine, No. CXXI, Vol. XXIII, pp. 50–51.
The Arts and Crafts of India and Ceylon. Edinburgh and London: Foulis, pp. 225.
Thirty Songs from the Punjab and Kashmir. (With an Introduction by the Translator and a Foreword by Rabindranath Tagore.) London: Luzac and Novello.

1914

Myths of the Hindus and the Buddhists. (In collaboration with Sister Nivedita.) London: George G. Harrap Ltd.
"The Eight Nayikas." *Journal of Indian Art,* No. 16, pp. 100–112.
"Notes on Jaina Art." *Journal of Indian Art,* No. 16, pp. 81–98.
Bronzes from Ceylon (Chiefly in the Colombo Museum) Mem. Colombo Museum. Series A, No. 1.
Visvakarma (First Series). (One Hundred Examples of Indian Architecture, Sculpture, Painting and Handicraft, with an Introduction by Eric Gill), London: Luzac and Co.
Hands and Feet in Indian Art, The Burlington Magazine. Vol. XXIV, No. CXXX, pp. 204–211.

1915

The Taking of Toll. London: Old Bourne Press.
Vidyapati: Bangiya Padavali, Songs of the Love of Radha and Krishna. (In collaboration with Arun Sen) London: Old Bourne Press.
"What Has India Contributed to Human Welfare?" *The Athenaeum.* No. 4588, Supplement, pp. 7.

The Gods of Mahayana Buddhism. The Burlington Magazine. Vol. XXVII, No. CXLVIII, pp. 139–141.

"Love and Art. *The Modern Review* (May), pp. 574–580. Calcutta.

"That Beauty is a State." *The Burlington Magazine,* Vol. XXVII, No. CXLV, pp. 7–14.

1916

Buddha and the Gospel of Buddhism. London: George Harrap and Co., and New York: Putnam and Co. pp. viii–370. Plates: 40, including eight in color by Abanindranath Tagore and Nandalal Bose.

Rajput Painting, Oxford, University Press.

"Buddhist Primitives." *The Burlington Magazine,* Vol. XXVIII, No. CLIV, pp. 151–155; No. CLVI, pp. 224–230.

1917

The Mirror of Gesture. From the Sanskrit *Abhinayadarpana* of Nandi-keshvara. (In collaboration with G. K. Duggirala), Cambridge, Mass.: Harvard University Press.

"Illustrated Jaina Manuscripts" *Bulletin of the Boston Museum of Fine Arts.* Vol. XV, No. 90, pp. 40–41.

"Oriental Dances in America," *Vanity Fair* (May).

1918

The Dance of Shiva: Fourteen Indian Essays. New York: Sunwise Turn. Introduction by Romain Rolland.

"Indian Bronzes." *Bulletin of the Boston Museum of Fine Arts,* Vol. XVI, No. 95, pp. 31–41.

"Rajput Painting." *Bulletin of the Boston Museum of Fine Arts,* Vol. XVI, No. 96, pp. 49–62.

1919

"Portrait of Gosain Jadrup." *Journal of the Royal Asiatic Society,* pp. 389–391.

"Indian Stone Sculptures." *Bulletin of the Boston Museum of Fine Arts,* Vol. XVII, No. 104, pp. 57–63.

"Buddhist Art in Asia: Its Origin and Development." *Asia Magazine,* Vol. XIX, No. 4, pp. 353–360.

1920

"The Rasikapriya of Keshavadasa." *Bulletin of the Boston Museum of Fine Arts,* Vol. XVIII, No. 109, pp. 50–52.

"A Nepalese Buddhist Painting." *Bulletin of the Boston Museum of Fine Arts,* Vol. XVIII, No. 106, pp. 14–17.

"Siamese Bronzes." *Ibid.,* pp. 17–20.

"Khmer Sculpture." *Ibid.,* p. 21.

"Art and Craftsmanship." *Dial*, LXVIII, pp. 744-746.

1921

"Sculptures civaites," (Saiva Sculptures). (In collaboration with A.
   Rodin, E. B. Havell and V. Goloubew). Brussels and Paris, Van Oest.
   Ars Asiatica, III, 31.
"Notes on the Javanese Theatre," *Rupam*, (July), No. 7, pp. 5-11.
   Calcutta.

1922

"Saiva Sculptures." *Bulletin of the Boston Museum of Fine Arts,* Vol.
   XX, No. 118, pp. 16-24.
"Recent Acquisitions of the Department of Indian Art," *Bulletin of the
   Boston Museum of Fine Arts,* Vol. XX, No. 122, pp. 69-73.

1923

Catalogue of Indian Art. Boston Museum of Fine Arts. Part I: General
   Introduction; Part II: Sculpture.
"Medieval and Modern Hinduism." (In collaboration with Stella Bloch)
   Asia Magazine, Vol. XXIII, No. 3, pp. 203-206, 230.
"America and India." *Orient,* Vol. I, No. 1, pp. 15-17. New York.
"Modern Indian Artists." *Orient,* Vol. I, No. 4, pp. 49-50. New York.
Introduction to Indian Art. Adyar, Madras: Theosophical Publishing
   House. (Asia Library Series).
Portfolio of Indian Art. Boston Museum of Fine Arts.

1924

"Todi Ragini," (Poem in Hindi, anonymous). *The New Orient,* Vol. II,
   No. 1, p. 36.
"Ragmala Poems," *Ibid.,* pp. 76-78.
Les Arts et Metiers de l'Inde et de Ceylan. Paris: Vromant.
Jaina Paintings and Manuscripts. Boston Museum of Fine Arts.
"Buddhist Sculpture." *Bulletin of the Boston Museum of Fine Arts,* Vol.
   XXII, No. 132, p. 30.

1925

"Three Fragments of Gandhara Sculpture." *Bulletin of the Boston
   Museum of Fine Arts,* Vol. XXIII, No. 140, pp. 73-75.

1926

Pour comprendre l'art Hindou. Paris, Bossard.
"Early Indian Sculptures." *Bulletin of the Boston Museum of Fine Arts,*
   Vol. XXIV, No. 144, pp. 54-60.
"Rajput Paintings." *Ibid.,* No. 142, pp. 23-26.

1927

"Notes on Indian Paintings: A Contribution to Mughal Iconography,"
Artibus Asiae, No. 1, pp. 5–11.

"A Pallava Early Relief." *Bulletin of the Boston Museum of Fine Arts,*
Vol. XXV, No. 148.

"A Hamsalakshana Sari." *Ibid.,* No. 149, pp. 36–37.

"Sculptures from Mathura." *Ibid.,* No. 150, pp. 50–54.

"Early Indian Terracottas." *Ibid.,* No. 152, pp. 90–96.

"The Task Before Us." *Oriental Magazine,* Vol. I, No. 2, p. 34.

History of Indian and Indonesian Art. New York. Weyhe. German Edition: Leipzig, Hiersemann.

"Sthanam." *Journal of the Royal Asiatic Society,* p. 322.

"Two Sunga Railing Pillars." *Ibid.,* p. 847.

"Relation of Mughal and Rajput Painting." *Rupam,* No. 31, pp. 88–91. Calcutta.

"The Origin of the Buddha Image." *Art Bulletin,* No. 9, pp. 287–317.

1928

"Indian Architectural Terms." *Journal of the American Oriental Society.* No. 48, pp. 250–275.

"An Early Khmer Head of Vishnu." *Bulletin of the Boston Museum of Fine Arts,* Vol. XXVI, No. 153, pp. 16–17.

"Notes on Indian Coins and Symbols." *Ostasiatische Zeitschr.* (N.F.), No. 4, pp. 175–188.

"*Yakshas.*" Washington: Smithsonian Institute. *Miscellaneous Collection,* Vol. 80, No. 6, p. 43.

"Hindu Ideals of Marriage." *Oriental Magazine,* Vol. II, No. 1, pp. 19–24.

"Ganesha." *Bulletin of the Boston Museum of Fine Arts,* Vol. XXVI, No. 154, pp. 629–630.

"Ekapatra Nagaraja." *Journal of the Royal Asiatic Society,* pp. 629–630.

"The Buddha's Chuda." (Hair, Ushnisha, Crown), *Ibid.,* pp. 815–841.

"Some Early Buddhist Reliefs Identified." *Ibid.,* pp. 390–398.

1929

"Andhra Sculptures." *Bulletin of the Boston Museum of Fine Arts,* Vol. XXVII, No. 160, pp. 20–23.

"A Very Ancient Indian Seal." *Ibid.,* pp. 28–29.

"An Early Cambodian Statue of Harihara." *Ibid.,* No. 161, pp. 40–41.

"A Yakshi Torso from Sanchi." *Ibid.,* No. 164, pp. 90–94.

"Picture Showmen." *Indian Historical Quarterly,* No. 5, pp. 182–187.

"A Chinese Buddhist Water-Vessel and Its Prototype." (In collaboration with F. S. Kershaw), *Artibus Asiae,* No. 3, pp. 122–143.

"Nagara Painting." *Rupam,* No. 37, pp. 24–29. Calcutta.

"Buddhist Reliefs from Nagarjunakonda and Amaravati." *Rupam,* Nos. 38–39, pp. 70–78. Calcutta.
"The Tree of Jesse and Indian Parallels of Sources." *Art Bulletin,* II, 218–220.

1930·

"Two Pallava Marble Pillars." *Bulletin of the Boston Museum of Fine Arts,* Vol. XXVIII, No. 167, pp. 55–58.
"A Pastoral Paradise." *Ibid.,* No. 168, pp. 64–65.
"The Shadow Play in Ceylon." *Journal of the Royal Asiatic Society,* 1930, p. 627.
"Two Leaves from a 17th Century Manuscript of Rasikapriya." *Metropolitan Museum Studies,* III, pp. 14–21. New York.
"One Hundred References to Indian Painting." *Artibus Asiae,* Vol. IV, No. 1, pp. 41–57.

1931

"The Gods of India." In *The Golden Book of Tagore,* Calcutta.
"The 'Webbed Finger' of the Buddha." *Indian Historical Quarterly,* VII, 365–366.
"Yakshas." (Part II), *Publication no. 3059.* Washington: Smithsonian Institute.
"A Stucco Head from Central Asia." *Bulletin of the Boston Museum of Fine Arts,* Vol. XXIX, No. 173, pp. 39–43.
"Two Western Indian Manuscripts." *Ibid.,* No. 171, pp. 4–11.
"A Yakshi Bust from Bharhut." *Ibid.,* No. 175, pp. 81–83.

1932

Introduction to the Art of Eastern Asia. Chicago: New Oriental Society. Monograph Series no. 2.
"The Mystery of Mahadeva." *Indian Art and Letters.* Vol. VI, No. 1, pp. 10–13.
"An Early Rajput Painting." *Bulletin of the Boston Museum of Fine Arts.* Vol. XXX, No. 179.
"A Vaishnava Relief." *Ibid.,* Vol. XXX, No. 178.
"A Bengali Painting." *Ibid.,* Vol. XXX, No. 179.

1933

"On Translation: Maya, Deva, Tapas." *Isis,* Vol. XIX, No. 55.
"Indian Sculpture at Zayton." *Ostasiatische Zeitschr.* (N.F.), IX, pp. 5–11.
A New Approach to the Vedas: An Essay in Translation and Exegesis. London: Luzac & Co.
"A Relief from Persepolis." *Bulletin of the Boston Museum of Fine Arts.* Vol. XXXI, pp. 22–25.

"Mahapralaya and the Last Judgment." *Indian Historical Quarterly,* Vol. IX.

"Versions from the Vedas." *Indian Art and Letters,* Vol. VII, No. 1, pp. 19–26.

1934

" 'Kha' and Other Words Denoting Zero, in Connection with the Metaphysics of Space." *Bulletin of the School of Oriental Studies,* VII, 487–497.

"Kwaja Khadir and the Fountain of Life, in the Tradition of Persian and Mughal Art." *Ars Islamica,* I, 173–182.

"The Technique and Theory of Indian Painting." *Technical Studies,* III, 59–89.

"Understanding the Art of India." *Parnassus,* Vol. VI, No. 4.

1935

"Angel and Titan: An Essay in Vedic Ontology." *Journal of the American Oriental Society,* No. 55, pp. 373–419.

Elements of Buddhist Iconography. Cambridge: Harvard University Press.

Mediaeval Aesthetic (Part I): *Dionysius the Pseudo-Areopagite and Ulrich Engelberti of Strasburg.* Art Bulletin, No. 17, pp. 31–47.

The Rigveda as Land-Nama-Bok. London: Luzac & Co.

"La Sculpture de Bodhgaya." *Ars Asiatica:* XVIII, 72

"A Study of the Katha Upanishad." *Indian Historical Quarterly,* II, 570–584.

The Transformation of Nature in Art. Cambridge: Harvard University Press.

"The Darker Side of Dawn." *Miscellaneous Collections.* No. 94. Washington: Smithsonian Institute.

1936

"The Nature of 'Folklore' and 'Popular Art.' " *Quarterly Journal of the Mythic Society,* No. 27, pp. 1–12.

Patron and Artist: Pre-Renaissance and Modern (In collaboration with A. Graham Carey). Norton, Mass.: Wheaton College Press.

"Rebirth and Omniscience in Pali Buddhism." *Indian Culture,* No. III, pp. 19–33.

"Vedic Exemplarism." *Harvard Journal of Asian Studies,* No. 1, pp. 44–64.

"Two Passages in Dante's 'Paradiso.' " *Speculum,* II, pp. 327–338.

"Vedic Monotheism." *Journal of Indian History,* No. 15, pp. 84–92.

"Sri Ramakrishna and Religious Tolerance." *Prabuddha Bharata,* June, pp. 268–74. Mayavati, India.

"Appreciation of the Unfamiliar Arts." *Vishwabharati Quarterly,* Vol. II, Part I, pp. 17–21.

"On the Pertinence of Philosophy." In *Contemporary Indian Philosophy,* edited by S. Radhakrishnan and J. H. Muirhead. London: George Allen and Unwin.

"An Indian Crocodile." *Bulletin of the Boston Museum of Fine Arts,* Vol. XXXIV, No. 202.

1937

"Pantheism, Indian and Platonic." *Journal of Indian History,* No. 16, pp. 249–252.

"The Part of Art in Indian Life." *Cultural Heritage of India,* III, pp. 255–359. Calcutta.

Is Art a Superstition or a Way of Life? (Lecture at the Metropolitan Museum, New York). Newport, R.I.: J. Stevens.

"The Indian Doctrine of Man's Last End." *Asia Magazine* (May), pp. 380–381.

"Christianity and Hinduism. *Ibid.,* p. 396.

"The Pilgrim's Way." *Journal of the Bihar and Orissa Research Society.* No. 23, pp. 452–471.

What Use Is Art, Anyway? Newport, R.I.: J. Stevens.

"The Vedic Doctrine of Silence." *Indian Culture,* No. 3, pp. 559–569.

"Janaka and Yajnavalkya." *Indian Historical Quarterly,* XIII, pp. 261–278.

1938

"The Inverted Tree." *Quarterly Journal of the Mythic Society,* No. 29. pp. 111–149.

"Asiatic Art." *Journal of New Oriental Society.* Chicago.

"Mediaeval Aesthetics." (Part II), *Art Bulletin,* No. 20, pp. 66–77.

"The Philosophy of Mediaeval and Oriental Art." *Zamoxis,* I, 2–49.

"The Symbolism of the Dome." *Indian Historical Quarterly,* No. 14, pp. 1–56.

"Tathagata." *Bulletin of the School of Oriental Studies,* IX, 331.

"The Tantrik Doctrine of Divine Biunity." *Annals of the Bhandarkar Oriental Research Institute,* No. 19, pp. 173–183.

"Nirmana-kaya." *Journal of the Royal Asiatic Society,* pp. 81–84. 1938.

1939

"Mediaeval Aesthetics: On the Relation of Beauty to Truth" Art Notes. March/April, pp. 55–57.

The Christian and Oriental, or True Philosophy of Art. Newport, R.I.: J. Stevens.

"Vedanta and the Western Tradition." *American Scholar,* pp. 223–247.

"The Reinterpretation of Buddhism." *New Indian Antiquary*, 11, 9, pp. 575–590.
"Mahatma." In *Mahatma Gandhi: Essays and Reflections,* edited by S. Radhakrishnan, pp. 63–67.
"An Indian Ivory." *Bulletin of the Boston Museum of Fine Arts,* Vol. XXXVII, No. 221, p. 51.

1940

"Primitive Mentality." *Quarterly Journal of the Mythic Society,* XXXI, pp. 69–91.
"The Nature of Mediaeval Art." *Art News,* 1940.
"Marco Pallis: 'Peaks and Lamas.' " *Asia Magazine,* XL, No. 2, p. 111.
"Akimchana: 'Self-naughting.' " *New Indian Antiquary,* III, 1–16.

1941

"Lila." *Journal of the American Oriental Society,* No. 61, pp. 98–101.
"Measures of Fire." *Oriental Institute.* No. 100, pp. 386–395.
"An Ivory Casket from Southern India." *Art Bulletin.* Vol. XXIII, No. 4, pp. 207–212.
"G. H. Hardy: 'A Mathematician's Apology.' " *Art Bulletin.* Vol. XXIII, No. 4, p. 339.

1942

Spiritual Authority and Temporal Power in the Indian Theory of Government. New Haven, Conn.: American Oriental Society, Series 22.
"On Being in One's Right Mind." *Review of Religion.* No. 7, 32–40.
"Eric Gill: 'Autobiography.' " *Journal of Aesthetics and Art-Criticism.* Vol. V.
"Eastern Religions and Western Thought." *Review of Religion,* VI, pp. 129–145.
"Why Exhibit Works of Art?" *Blackfriars* (September, 1942), pp. 358–363.
"Atmayajna: Self-sacrifice." *Harvard Journal of Asian Studies,* VI, pp. 358–398.

1943

Hinduism and Buddhism. New York: Philosophical Library, VIII, 86.
"Eastern Wisdom and Western Knowledge." *Isis,* XXXIV, 359–363.
"Am I My Brother's Keeper?" *Asia and the Americas,* No. 43, pp. 135–138.

1944

"Recollection, Indian and Platonic and The One and Only Transmigrant." *Journal of American Oriental Society.* Supplement, pp. 1–80.

"The Symbolism of Archery." *Ars Islamica,* X, 105-119.
"Paths That Lead to the Same Summit." *Motive* (May, 1944), pp. 29-32.
"The Bugbear of Literacy." *Asia and the Americas,* 1944, pp. 53-57.
"Gradation and Evolution." *Isis,* XXXV, 15-16.

1945

"Imitation, Expression and Participation." *Journal of Aesthetics and Art-Criticism,* III, 62-72.
"East and West." *Biosophical Review,* VIII, No. 1, pp. 15-18.
"Spiritual Paternity" and "Puppet Complex." *Psychiatry,* VIII, 287-297.

1946

"Figures of Speech and Figures of Thought." In *Collected Essays on the Traditional View of Art.* London. Luzac & Co.
"For What Heritage and To Whom Are the English-speaking Peoples Responsible?" *Kenyon College Conference Volume,* pp. 48-65.
"The Feudal Craftsman in India and Ceylon. *Shilpi,* Vol. I, No. 5, pp. 16-26. Madras.
Am I My Brother's Keeper? (A collection of Essays) New York: John Day & Co.

1947

Time and Eternity. Ascona, Switzerland: Artibus Asiae Publishers.
"India's Renaissance." *The Hindu,* Independence Day Number. Madras.
"Myths and Symbols in Indian Art and Civilisation." (A Review of the book by Heinrich Zimmer) *Review of Religion,* March, 1947.

ADDENDA

Articles in the *Encyclopaedia Britannica,* 14th Edition, Chicago, 1929.
Indian and Simhalese Art and Archaeology.
Indonesian and Further Indian Art.
Indian Architecture.
Bronze and Brass, Indian and Indonesian
Textiles and Embroideries, Indian and Indonesian
Yakshas

Articles in the *National Encyclopaedia,* New York, 1932.
Indian Architecture
Indian Art

Contribution to *Websters' International Dictionary.* 1934. Edited all words of Indian origin.

Contributions to *Dictionary of World Literature,* edited by Joseph T. Shipley. New York, 1943.
Indian Drama
Indian Literary Theatre
Symbolism
Ornament

POSTHUMOUS PUBLICATIONS

The Living Thoughts of Gotama, the Buddha. (In collaboration with H. J. Horner) London: Cassell & Co., 1948.

"Buddhism." In *Religion in the Twentieth Century,* edited by Vergilius Ferm. New York: Philosophical Library, 1948.

The Bugbear of Literacy. Collected essays, with an Introduction by Robert A. Parker. london: Dennis Dobston Ltd., 1949.

"Note on the Philosophy of Persian Art." *Ars Islamica,* Nos. XV-XVI, 1950.

The Wisdom of Ananda Coomaraswamy. Thoughts, selected from his writings, letters and speeches by S. Durai Raja singam. With an Introduction by Whitehall N. Perry. Published by S. Durai Raja Singam from Petaling Jaya, Malaysia.

A University Course in Indian Art. Lectures at the Metropolitan Museum, New York. Based on notes taken by Dr. Marguerite B. Block, and edited by S. Durai Raja Singam. Published by S. Durai Raja Singam.

BOOKS AND ARTICLES ABOUT ANANDA K. COOMARASWAMY

Art and Thought. Essays in honor of Ananda K. Coomaraswamy presented on his 70th birthday. Edited by K. Bharatha Iyer. London: Luzac & Co., 1947.

Homage to Kalayogi Ananda Coomaraswamy. A 70th Birthday Volume. Edited by S. Durai Raja Singam. Kuantan, Malaya, 1947.

Ananda Coomaraswamy. By D. P. Dhanapala, in *Eminent Indians.* Bombay: Nalanda Publications, 1947.

I Meet Dr. Ananda Coomaraswamy. By S. Chandrashekhara, in *Aryan Path,* Vol. XVIII, No. 8, pp. 364-371.

In Memoriam: Ananda Coomaraswamy. By Murray Fowler, in *Artibus Asiae,* Vol. X, No. 3.

Ananda Coomaraswamy. By Swami Jagadishvarananda, in *Modern Review,* January, 1948.

Some Recollections and References. By Dona Luisa Coomaraswamy in *Kalamanjari,* Colombo, 1950.

Remembering and Remembering, Again and Again. A Tribute to

Kalayogi Ananda Coomaraswamy in Words and Pictures. Edited by S. Durai Raja Singam and published by him from Petaling Jaya, Malaysia.

Selected Glossary

Ābhāsa: 'Shining back'; semblance.

Abhyāsa: Practice, training.

Achārya: A master; an expert in some art.

Adhyāsa: Imposition by the mind of the nature of one thing upon another. Especially the imposition of finite attributes on the Infinite.

Advaita: Non-dualistic.

Ahamkāra: Ego-sense.

Ākāsha: Space.

Alamkāra: Ornament; associated ideas in poetry.

Ādhyātma-vidyā: The science of self-realization.

Alaukika: Trans-phenomenal.

Ālaya Vijnāna: Storehouse-consciousness.

Amritattva: Immortality.

Ānanda: Joy.

Antarjneya: Subjectively known.

Anukriti: Aesthetic imitation.

Ardhanārīshvara: The Divine represented as half male and half female.

Artha: Meaning; fame and prosperity, one of the four objectives of life recognized in Hinduism.

Asmitā: Sense of one's own personality.

Āsvāda: Tasting, especially tasting of aesthetic delight.

Ātman: The Supreme Self.

Avatāra: Appearance of the Divine in phenomenal, especially human, form.

Avidyā: Cosmic ignorance.

Bhāva: Feeling or mood expressed in art; a vehicle of *rasa* (see *rasa*)

Bhakti: Devotion to and love of God.

Bhikshu: A Buddhist monk.

Bhūtātman: Individual soul (as distinguished from Ātman, the Supreme Spirit)

Bodhisattva: 'Enlightenment-essence.'

Brahman: Ultimate Reality. The Unconditioned.

Buddhi: Intellect.

Chitta: Mind.

Chitta-vritti: Modifications of the Spirit by the mind.

Chitra: Picture.

Darshana: Perspective. Viewpoint. A philosophical system.

Dharana: Exclusive concentration.

Dharma: Conduct. Morality. The essential characteristic of a thing.

Dharmaparyāya: Divergent formulations of Dharma.

Dhvani: Sound. Overtone of meaning.
Divya: Divine.

Ekam: The One.

Grahana: 'Seizing.' Comprehension.
Guna: Attribute. A constituent element of Nature in Sāmkhya philosophy.
Guru: Teacher. Spiritual preceptor.

Harsha: Delight.

Ichchāshakti: The power of desire.
Ishvara: God. In Vedanta philosophy, the Absolute in its manifest aspect.

Jina: Conqueror, especially one who conquers his lower nature.
Jīva: The finite self.
Jīvanmukta: Liberated while alive.

Kāma: Pleasure. One of the four objectives of life recognized in Hinduism.
Kārana: Cause.
Karma: Deed. Action. The accumulated consequences of one's deeds in successive lifetimes.
Karmaphala: Fruit of one's action.
Kārya: Effect.
Kaushala: Skill.
Kāvya: Poetry.
Kha: Sky. Cosmic space.
Kīrtana: A devotional song, usually sung by a group.

Lakshana: Sign. Characteristic lineament of an image (in sculpture).
Līlā: Play, Sport, especially divine sport.
Lokottara: World-transcending.

Mahat: 'The Great One,' same as Buddhi, the first product of evolution in Samkhya philosophy.
Manas: Mind. Psyche.
Mantra: A mystical couplet or formula, supposed to possess spiritual efficacy.
Māyā: Illusion. World-appearance.
Moksha: Emancipation. Liberation from the wheel of birth-and-death.
Mukti: Same as Moksha.
Mūrta: Embodied.

Nāma-rūpa: 'Name and form,' i.e. the empirical personality.
Nirmāna: Creation. Construction.
Niyama: Rule. Regulation. Discipline.
Nritya: Dance.

Pāramārthika: Transcendental. Metaphysical.
Prajnā: Insight. Pure intellect.
Prakriti: Nature. The material world.

Pramāna: Proof. Proportion.
Prāna: Life-breath.
Pratibimba: Reflection. Aesthetic representation.
Pratīka: Symbol.
Pratyaksha: Actual. Perception as a source of knowledge.
Pūjā: Worship through ritual.
Purusha: The spiritual principle (as distinct from Prakriti, the material principle).
Purushartha(s): The four objectives of life recognized in Hinduism.

Rāga: A melodic pattern in Indian music.
Rasa: Aesthetic flavor or mood.
Rita: The principle of order and rhythm governing the universe.
Rūpa: Form.
Rupa-bhedah: The differentiation of forms in a work of art.

Sādharanīkarana: The universalization of a mood or emotion through aesthetic expression.
Sādrishya: The concomittance of formal and pictorial elements in art.
Sahridaya: "Man with a heart," i.e. a spiritually or imaginatively gifted person.
Sat: The Real.
Sattva: The element of purity and knowledge in all things; one of the three constitutive elements in Prakriti or Nature.
Satya: Truth.
Shakti: The principle of creativity and energy, an aspect of the Real distinct from the aspect of Pure Existence and Consciousness.
Shilpa: Craft.
Shithila-samādhi: Imperfect concentration (of the artist).
Shūnya: Void. Emptiness. Transcendental Reality.
Sthāyībhāva: The enduring feeling in aesthetic experience.
Stūpa: A funerary mound erected over the enshrined relics of the Buddha or his important disciples.
Sūtra: A scriptural or authoritative text, usually a collection of aphoristic statements.
Svabhāva: One's own nature.
Svadharma: Own's own duty.
Svapnavat: Dreamlike.
Svarūpa: One's own form.
Svayamprakāsha: Self-luminous.

Tadekam: That which is One.
Tat: That (The Absolute in its essential nature, which is indescribable.)
Tathatā: 'Thatness.'
Tathāgata: He who has arrived at Thatness. One of the epithets of the Buddha.

Vana-devatā: A forest deity, a wood-nymph.
Varnikābhanga: Distribution of color in a painting.
Vishvakarmā: The World-architect.
Vyanjanā: Aesthetic suggestiveness.

Yajna: A religious sacrifice with ritual and chanting of hymns.
Yoga: Union. 'Yoking.' A spiritual discipline leading to self-realization and liberation.

Index

COLDSMITH, Don
Child of the dead